AF593974
9780238789809

Stern End of a Motor Boat, Stoke Bruerne (1967)

Canal Boats and Boaters

D.J. Smith

Hugh Evelyn London

First published in 1973 by
Hugh Evelyn Ltd
9 Fitzroy Square, London W1P 5AH

SBN 238.78980.2

Designed by Richard Moon

Printed in Great Britain by
Balding and Mansell

Contents

Acknowledgements

The author wishes to thank the following for their help and co-operation in compiling this book.

British Waterways Board
R. J. Hutchings Esq.
The Curator and Staff of the Waterways Museum
J. Fenton Esq.
Members of the Birmingham Canal Navigation Society
L. R. Hogg Esq.
Miss G. M. Crowe
Miss B. Abbott
T. Lewery Esq.
M. LeRoy Esq.
P. A. Stevens Esq. MA, FMA
The Railway and Canal Historical Society
J. A. Daniell Esq.
Brian J. Collings Esq. (especially for advice concerning illustrations)
Sheila Hutchins of the *Daily Express*
T. A. Walden Esq. Director of Leicester Museums
D. Owen Esq. Director of the Manchester Museum
G. Postles Esq.
K. Bennett Esq. (especially for photographs and advice concerning illustrations)

Introduction

We humans are strange beings: only has there to be the threat that some part of our heritage could disappear for a revival of interest to show itself. There is no clearer instance of this than the case of our own waterways where, despite the almost complete disappearance of narrow boat carrying, interest in boats and boat-people, so often referred to as 'barges' and 'bargees', is ever increasing. During any week I talk to many visitors to our museum at Stoke Bruerne and most of their questions seek to learn something about boat people, their way of living, their way of work and their floating homes.

Rivers were used for transport long before the cutting of man-made navigations but the story of our canal system began only a little more than 200 years ago. The St Helens Canal in south Lancashire, partly opened in 1757 to carry coal to the Mersey and up the River Weaver to the salt industries located there, antedates by four years the more famous Bridgewater Canal from the Duke of Bridgewater's coal mines at Worsley into Manchester. Between 1761 and 1820 many immense waterways were cut linking Mersey, Trent, Severn and Thames. There were canals in Scotland, in Wales, deep into the south-west and south-east country and by the 1820s a vast network had been completed. But for another 20 years the network was improved by additions such as Telford's Caledonian Canal and his straight waterway from Nantwich to Wolverhampton. They carried immense quantities of coal, ironstone, finished goods, ironwork for factories, building materials, timber, stone for pavements and roads. They carried the coal and lime the countryside needed and brought back agricultural produce to the towns. Many millions of tons a year were moved and while the better-situated canals were prosperous others failed. Their prosperity was relatively short. In the 1820s the first railways were built but their coming made little immediate difference to canals which were still the cheapest form of transport and much of the material needed to build railways was, ironically, carried on the waterways.

There were great factors in favour of the railways. The more important canals were congested, so congested that they could not carry more traffic without reconstruction. Again, immense waterborne traffic created water shortage.

Operation in a hilly country like ours where canals are heavily locked is expensive in water and many companies were desperate for adequate supplies, a state of affairs which led to traffic delay. Much canal traffic was lost to the railways and their coming started the slow decline. Some canal companies spent a great deal of money on modernisation but most could not raise the cash needed with their falling traffic and the general movement of industry in favour of the new railways.

At first the family boat was rare and most narrow boats were crewed by men whose families lived ashore, but when carriers were forced to cut their rates to meet rail competition their earnings went down heavily. The narrow boatmen economised by dispensing with their crews and their houses ashore, and brought their families on to the boats to live and to work. By carrying his family with him the boatman saved the cost of maintaining his cottage.

Thomas Monk of Tipton and Stourport, born in 1765, a power in canal carrying, was the inventor and first builder of the small canal cabin-boat with accommodation for the boatman and his wife. Thomas Monk's boats were known as 'monkey boats' a nick-name still surviving in the canal boat world.

This method of running his boat was first adopted by the self-employed boatman, known as a 'number one', and later taken up by the firms of canal carriers who owned fleets of boats and employed the boatmen. Very briefly this is how the family boat came into being.

It has been suggested that boating families were of gipsy extraction, a suggestion they disliked intensely and one founded only on a vague similarity between the boat cabin, with its decorations of lace, polished brass work and paintwork, and the Romany caravan. They were hardworking people who ate, slept, lived and brought up their families in the confined space of a cabin only about 7 ft. wide and 10 ft. long. They established a closely knit community, intermarrying, and with it all a long-lasting tradition for decorative work, colourful painting inside and outside their boats, their water-cans, horse bowls, dippers, lamps, stools and in fact any suitable surface being coloured with one design or another.

They toiled through bleak winters, coping with icy locks and dreary tunnels, and they were patient people, they must have been or how else would they have tolerated their way of living, one day like the other, its monotony unrelieved, its tale of work unchanged.

In 1922, there were still over 12,000 canal boats registered as dwellings and probably three-fourths of that number were occupied continuously. Those tiny cabins compact with miniature fittings, the floating homes of a population equal in its aggregate to that of a medium-sized town of 50,000 persons.

The Waterways Museum at Stoke Bruerne, rich in pictures and exhibits, clearly shows the conditions in which boat people lived. Everyone on the 'cut' knew everyone else no matter where they were trading, and it was rare for an 'outsider' to be invited aboard a family boat.

This method of running canal narrow boats posed serious social problems and perhaps its worst feature was the denial of educational opportunity to the children. Some children did attend ordinary schools but because no boat was tied up for very long little success was accomplished. Some special schools were set up and, although standards obtained were low, they at least fulfilled a much-felt want. Few children were able to have continuous schooling and clearly the only method of providing for education was to keep boat children off the boats altogether during school term time. His children were much too useful to the boatman and this ideal was never achieved.

No craft on inland waterways or on any waterway could have been quite as gay and highly decorated as some of the narrow boats of pre-nationalisation days, and this includes the horses carrying their gay trappings amidst their harness. Whenever possible horses were stabled when the day's work was over; stables being found at many points along the canal system. They were built either by the canal companies or the carrying companies or by individuals. In the latter case, stables could be hired for an overnight stay. The enormous stable at Bunbury in Cheshire alongside the main line of the Shropshire Union Canal is typical and it stands alongside Bunbury Locks. The Shropshire Union Company was by far the greatest carrier on its own line and in 1905 owned over three hundred horses. The speed of the horse-drawn narrow boat was slow and one boat loaded pulled by one horse averaged only two miles an hour.

Donald Smith's book is about all these things and many more, but the reader must not be misled into thinking that all boats were that clean, compact, highly decorated picture which we emphasise at Stoke Bruerne Museum. One can imagine the 'lady of the boat' ever struggling to cook, to feed and clean her children, to clean her cabins and to do her share of running the boats, operating locks and the many other tasks which must have been her lot.

Sadly working boats are now a rare sight indeed but tradition will not disappear with them. There are too many canal enthusiasts, too many writers and researchers placing on record this fascinating story, for such a thing to happen.

I hope you will enjoy reading this book.

Waterways Museum
Stoke Bruerne

Richard Hutchings

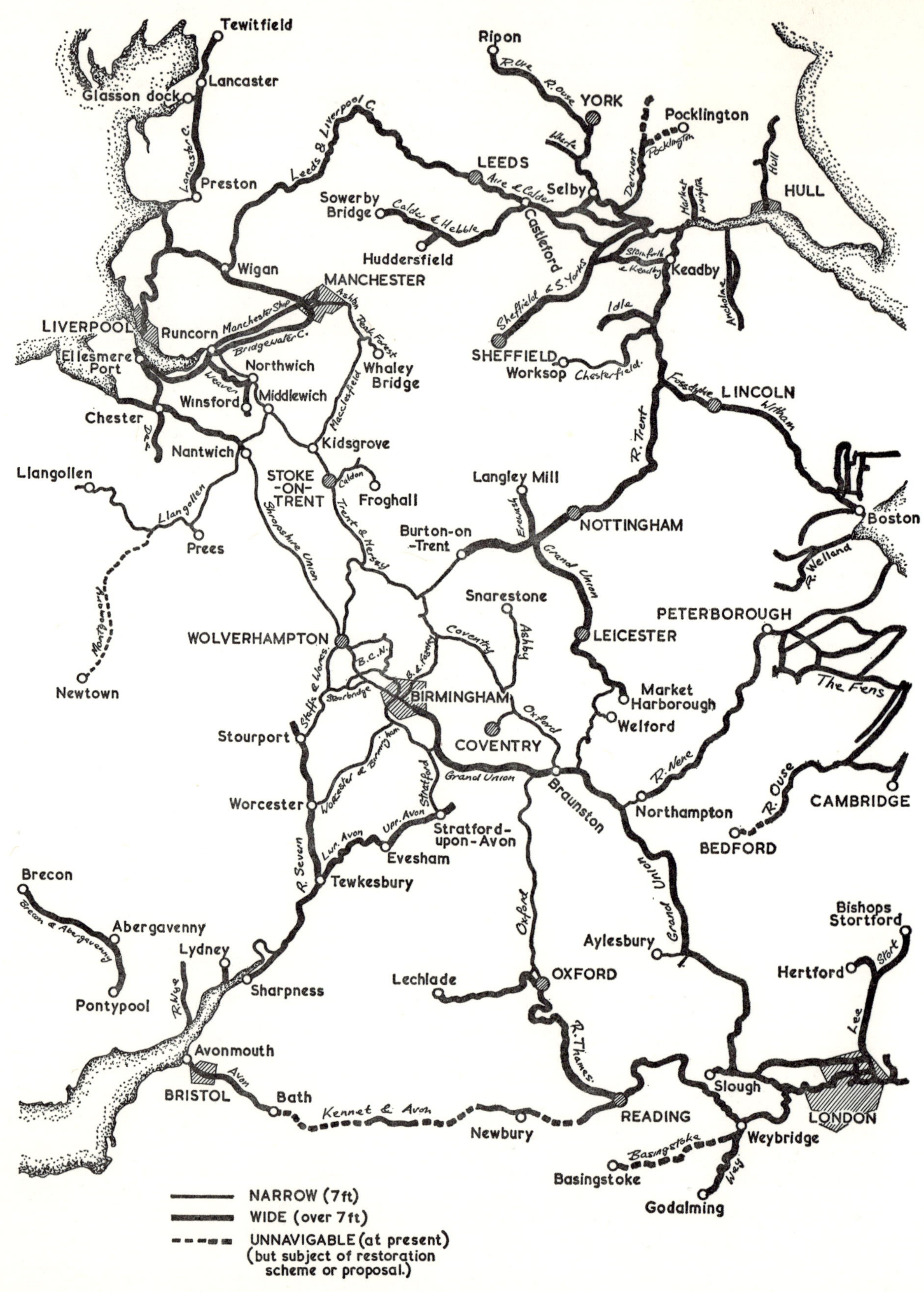

Tewitfield
Lancaster
Glasson dock
Lancaster C.
Preston
Leeds & Liverpool C.
Ripon
R. Ure
R. Ouse
YORK
Pocklington
Wharfe
Derwent
Pocklington
LEEDS
Aire & Calder
Selby
Sowerby Bridge
Calder & Hebble
Castleford
Huddersfield
Market Weighton
Hull
HULL
Wigan
MANCHESTER
Ashton
Peak Forest
Stainforth & Keadby
Keadby
Sheffield & S. Yorks
Ancholme
Idle
LIVERPOOL
Runcorn
Manchester Ship
Bridgewater C.
Ellesmere Port
Northwich
Whaley Bridge
SHEFFIELD
Worksop
Chesterfield
Fossdyke
LINCOLN
Witham
Weaver
Winsford
Middlewich
Macclesfield
Chester
Dee
Nantwich
Kidsgrove
R. Trent
Llangollen
STOKE-ON-TRENT
Caldon
Froghall
Langley Mill
Boston
Llangollen
Prees
Shropshire Union
Trent & Mersey
Erewash
NOTTINGHAM
Burton-on-Trent
Grand Union
R. Welland
Montgomery
Snarestone
Ashby
PETERBOROUGH
WOLVERHAMPTON
Coventry
LEICESTER
B.C.N.
B. & Fazeley
Staffs & Worcs.
Stourbridge
BIRMINGHAM
The Fens
Newtown
Market Harborough
Oxford
Welford
Stourport
COVENTRY
Worcester & Birmingham
Stratford
Grand Union
Braunston
R. Nene
R. Ouse
Worcester
Upr. Avon
Northampton
CAMBRIDGE
Stratford-upon-Avon
Lwr. Avon
Evesham
Braunston
BEDFORD
Grand Union
R. Severn
Tewkesbury
Brecon
Brecon & Abergavenny
Abergavenny
Oxford
Bishops Stortford
Lydney
Aylesbury
Grand Union
Stort
Hertford
R. Wye
Sharpness
Lechlade
OXFORD
Pontypool
R. Thames
Lee
Avonmouth
Avon
BRISTOL
Bath
Kennet & Avon
Slough
READING
LONDON
Newbury
Weybridge
Basingstoke
Basingstoke
Wey
Godalming
NARROW (7ft)
WIDE (over 7ft)
UNNAVIGABLE (at present) (but subject of restoration scheme or proposal.)

Chapter 1 The Story of the Canal Folk

There are several conflicting theories about the origins of English canal folk. It is a traditional belief that they are descended from gipsy stock, although others claim an inheritance from bargemen who navigated rivers and tidal reaches before the construction of a canal network. A less romantic theory, supported by Eric de Maré and L. T. C. Rolt, traces their background to the English countryside, especially to villages near the centre of the system from which inland waterways radiated to main estuaries.

It is certain that the operation of a new system, which began seriously with the opening of the Bridgewater Canal in 1761, needed personnel to match. A new kind of construction demanded a pioneer labour force, and as England was then mainly agricultural it is obvious that many recruits would be of peasant stock seeking the betterment others found in town life or emigration. These typical country dwellers might later have been joined by traditional watermen or bargees, a few gipsy folk and numbers of people, from both town and country, displaced in an age of transition.

While much has been written concerning the intermarriage of canal families and their traditional way of life on the waterways, one frequently comes across those who gave up a variety of occupations to make a fresh start on the 'cut'. Former miners, factory workers, clerks and schoolmasters, to name only some of them, find both challenge and reward working a narrow boat through the English shires. Such people who 'came off the land', especially in later years, are converts to a faith in human values, willing to sacrifice obvious comforts and take a chance with more than superficial hardships. Even today the life of the waterways demands mental and physical stamina of a high order. Yet those who come to terms with such a life rarely seek other outlets or return to land habits, unless driven out through closures and sheer lack of trade.

It may be judged that a minority of new blood 'off the land' has been present almost as long as there have been inland waterways. Newcomers were constantly absorbed into the older community which appears to have been established, almost as a separate race, for at least 130 years. While the canal folk may offer an outward impression of clannishness they have been willing enough to meet on equal terms those who accept them without prejudice or false sentiment. Traditional attitudes are a condition of life; they are partly defensive, dating back to times when settled, superior folk of cottage, farm and suburb condemned boat families as 'water gipsies'.

The first men associated with the canal system, apart from planners and speculators, were those who actually dug the 'stinking ditch'. These were the navigation canal builders, the 'navvies', who earned a reputation for hard work and wild living, both the envy and terror of wide areas around. Their labours often survived the use and popularity of canals; their counterparts of the following century built the metalled roads and railways which helped to make waterways either obsolete or less widely used. Railway navvies of the mid-nineteenth century were like human machines, tough and headstrong but lacking many of the finer qualities. By the 1840s construction work had become highly specialised; a matter of routine plus stamina rather than resourcefulness. The canal navvies however had been far more versatile, able to cope with new problems as they arose on a scale without parallel since the Roman occupation. Even the cathedrals of the Middle Ages were matched by the aqueducts, lifts and tunnels of the canal age, the design of hand tools and the quality of labour having changed very little during four or five centuries. Although frequently superstitious and often illiterate the early navvies were considered a cut above the general run of farm workers, from whom many of their class emerged, while some may have broadened their horizons by work on river barges or in the coasting trade.

James Brindley

When James Brindley cut the Bridgewater Canal across the wilderness of Trafford Moss near Manchester he was almost certain to have employed gipsy labour, some of whom may have also worked for him in other parts of the country, finally taking to a boating life and manning a few of the early canal craft. The country round Manchester has been a favourite haunt of Romany tribes for centuries and this theory, while it remains interesting but unproved, forms a basis for one of the few possible links between canal folk and the gipsy race. While not ruling out the possibility that some gipsies may have joined the work gang for more than a few weeks, as some in other districts are known to have forsaken their nomadic life in favour of regular farming, these were doubtless a minority. It is to the influence of this group that we may ascribe the crafts of fortune-telling and herbal remedies, at which many canal navvies appear to have been highly skilled. A fancied resemblance between the painting of gipsy wagons and canal boats however is most unlikely as few gipsies of the late eighteenth century used wheeled transport, being tent dwellers and sleepers under hedges. When Romany folk began to use living vans on an extensive scale they may have been influenced by examples of canal narrow boats, then established on the waterways for upwards of 60 years. The so-called 'gipsy' love of colour, ornament and distinctive costume are traits fostered by many peasant races throughout Europe; they are also shared with the Cockney barrow boy and costermonger.

Canal folk themselves resent the title gipsy, although it was a label freely applied during the nineteenth century to anyone moving about the country as part of his way of life. Fairground or circus showmen, strolling players and market hucksters were frequently confused with families of genuine Romany origin. Yet most gipsies were even more introvert and closely knit than canal dwellers, with as great a delight in changing casual work to escape routine as in travel for its own sake. Although the life of a boater was far less overshadowed by discipline than that of a mill hand, he was part of an ordered system to a greater extent than any to which most gipsies would then commit themselves. Perhaps the most convincing link between gipsy and boater was through the matriarchal side of their domestic life; the womenfolk of both groups had to be tough and domineering in order to survive.

During the early part of their history it was a common error to confuse canal folk with men who worked barges over navigable rivers. Anyone remotely connected with boats and barges, even the uncouth 'bowhaulier', was called a 'bargee', often as a term of abuse. Yet river barges, much broader in the beam, have little in common with canal boats, being more in their element on the tidal waters which smaller craft seldom use. While the barge has a master or skipper and a small crew, its methods of navigation and the terms used to describe it are similar to those shared with deep water seamen. The crew of a canal boat usually consists of a captain and mate or a captain and his family, wife and family acting as crew. When living and working on their craft the latter are known as 'boatmen' or 'boaters'. The owner-boater is further known as a 'number one', the aristocrat of his chosen occupation, very few of whom survived the hardships of the period between the two world wars.

There have always been families living on canals, although river barges are almost exclusively a masculine world. The skills involved in handling a barge are frequently identical with those of seamanship, but the traditional boater is rarely on watch for long periods, nor is he or she involved in hazards of wind, tide and current. On the other hand negotiating lock flights, tunnels and lifts are tasks unknown to river bargemen. The barge master was also unacquainted, until later years, with the use of animals for towing. Where towing of barges was necessary, to pass shallows and rapids, for example, it was done by loutish 'bowhauliers' whose reputation for bad language and dishonesty rubbed off not only on barge crews but also on canal boaters and anyone remotely connected with waterways. Most canals in Britain were constructed with towing paths and planned from the beginning for work with horses, mules and even donkeys. The care of these beasts was part of the daily work of many boaters (until the widespread use of powered craft during the late 1920s) for which the country up-bringing of the first boat families must have proved a useful asset.

Almost as wide a gap exists between bargee and boater as between boater and gipsy. They move in different spheres and work over different routes, each with his own traditions and way of life to preclude permanent change from either canal to river or river to canal. The boater is certainly a law unto himself and in the course of time has evolved a way of life without parallel in the annals of folk culture. Barges, apart from a limited decoration of scrollwork at stem and stern, are mainly austere and free from ornament; but the need to decorate plays a much greater part in the domesticated background of the canal boater. The narrow boat is more than a place of work or means of livelihood, it is a floating home in which families were born, bred, married and finally carried to their last resting place. It is not perhaps surprising that day boats, a few of which still work between

Birmingham and the Black Country in the care of day workers or 'Joey boaters', are far less colourful and attractive than the more popular family boats. While the day boats have a small cabin for temporary shelter at meal times, the living quarters of a family boat are kitchen, bedroom and dining saloon combined, to be furnished accordingly.

During the early days of canals their owners and promoters were frequently little more than toll clerks, maintaining a watery turnpike which could be used by a number of independent carriers ranging from small local concerns and larger firms, some with vested interests in a particular industry, to the 'number ones', who rarely owned more than one or two boats. In later years canal companies also acquired craft and traded on their own account. The boats of larger firms, some worked as 'fly' or express services, were frequently manned by young or single men, a gay company celebrated in verse and song for their way with the girls, the use of their fists and their liking for a glass of 'grog'. A 'number one' or boater working for the smaller firms was more frequently an older man, sometimes with a wife and children sharing the confined space of his stern cabin.

In the early days of the industry, when profits were high and wages and working hours reasonable, many canal boatmen provided homes on the land for their wives and children to which, like sailors, they returned at intervals. Yet even in those days there were families afloat, if only temporarily or for the sake of company. There were no restrictions on the education of children or conditions under which women and children might be employed. Children could be of practical use from an early age and were much better employed in the open air than sweeping chimneys or crawling about mine shafts.

From the 1840s and 1850s however the prosperity of the inland waterways gradually declined. Through railway competition, mismanagement and other causes, the life of the average boater became much harder and less rewarding. Longer hours were expected for less pay and it was no longer possible for a boater to own a cottage on the land to which he might retire in old age. Family boats soon became not merely a social convenience but an economic necessity, and by the late 1860s boats operated by all-male crews, except for those working 'fly', were an exception.

As might be expected, canal boats, like houses or cottages, varied according to their tenants. Most were neat and orderly, despite harsh poverty and cramped conditions. There were always odd offenders who kept what were known as 'Rodney boats' or floating slums, but these were given a wide berth by other canal folk. If ever there was a classic example of a place for everything and everything in its place it could certainly be found in life on a canal boat.

Although there were more family boats than ever before on the canals of the 1840s and 1850s this was also the time of greatest hardship and misery for boat families. Reforms in other spheres of industrial life seemed to have passed them by, at least until the introduction of the *Canal Boats Act* of 1877. This not only required that canal craft be registered and inspected, but focused public attention on the worst abuses and hardships of the boater's life. Investigation proved that many boaters and their families were illiterate, underpaid, badly fed and frequently unmarried. It is perhaps a wonder that so many of the 100,000 men and women reputed to be living on canals at this period should have managed so well in their struggle to keep up not only appearances but also traditional loyalties and family ties.

That conditions gradually improved during the final quarter of the nineteenth century was mainly due to the work of George Smith, an ardent reformer of nonconformist background, who gave up a well-paid job in industry to champion the cause of the boat dwellers. His survey of life and work on English canals, *Our Canal Population* (1875), may well have overstated the case for reform but it paved the way for the long-needed improvements introduced two years later with the Act of 1877. Like many reformers George Smith pursued his arguments to illogical conclusions, but in so doing he awakened the public conscience. At one stage of his campaigns he attempted to ban women and children from living or working on canals. This however was resisted by the boaters and rejected by the authorities at all levels, although from 1877 each boat was limited in the number of adults and children it might carry.

For several years George Smith tramped the canal towing paths from the home counties to the industrial north, first hailed as a worthy ally but later dreaded as a busybody. The boaters themselves were not always co-operative and hid their children in nearby bushes rather than admit to overcrowding. Local authorities were a further stumbling block with neither means nor inclination to enforce their writ. A second *Canal Act*, of 1884, not only sought to improve general standards of hygiene where this was necessary but provided for full time inspectors under local boards to see that regulations were understood and carried out. Enforcement however was seldom needed; given the right opportunity boaters proved themselves as clean and intelligent as other sections of the public. The main difficulty in later years was to implement the *Education Acts* and see that all children received proper schooling. This problem was eventually solved by the establishment of boarding schools and hostels for the younger generation, allowing them to work on the canals during their ample holidays.

Traditional boaters frequently give the impression of belonging to a closed community, with their own diversions and social life. It cannot however be overstressed that this is not merely an anti-social attitude but the result of work patterns beyond either control or recognition. Although men and women might travel thousands of miles during 60 years of active service, they seldom move more than a few yards from lockside or towing path. The occasional holiday is an event to be celebrated on the grand scale with gifts and souvenirs for all the family, some handed down for generations. In many ways the boater is a foreigner in his own country, unacquainted with the talk and habits of landsmen and when not working staying on safe ground in a bar of the once numerous canalside inns. Favourite pastimes, from ninepins to 'ringing the bull'*, even opportunities for courting, were for many years related to the atmosphere of lockside taverns and their dance halls. Although free fights and bitter feuds are far from unknown, the average boater is a peaceable square-dealing type rather than a bully or 'tearaway'. From the heyday of the family boat during the 1870s the wife and mother tended to rule the roost, keeping her menfolk in strict order. It may be far from coincidence that

* A parlour game similar to pinning the tail on the donkey.

the worst brawls in former days occurred between 'Joey boaters'.

A matriarchal society existed for over a century, with strict taboos and even a measure of segregation between the sexes. Men and women rarely congregated together outside the family circle, either drinking or talking in exclusively male or female groups. This may have been in fine contrast with the less inhibited attitude of the few single men employed on 'fly' boats, working express trips between London, Birmingham and other centres. These light-hearted bachelors, young, fit and unhampered by family ties, were typical of life on the canals before their decline, when there were fewer family boats and a larger number of dependants lived ashore.

It should not be thought however that the average boater of later years is a dull sort of chap, or moody and introspective. Less influenced by outside amusements, he is resourceful enough to make his own, able to improvise in song and story and a talented performer on melodeon and mouth-organ. From the 1890s to the 1930s the melodeon was as much a piece of furniture in most cabins as stool or bunk. Singing and step-dancing are popular diversions, especially at weddings and family gatherings.

It is difficult to say whether boat families are religious folk. Most are at least nominal members of the Church of England, which frequently ran missions to the canals during the second half of the nineteenth century. A few claim to be staunch Roman Catholics, and whole families in Cheshire and the Potteries were at one period actively connected with nonconformist sects. It is probable that the faith and worship of canal folk is of a simple order, the kind experienced by many people in daily contact with nature. Survivors claim 'there are no atheists in a lifeboat', a sentiment that may well find a parallel in the reeking darkness of the Harecastle Tunnel.

Concerning the inner man, the average boater, especially in later years, fared well by country standards. A busy outdoor life creates a keen appetite and a need for freshly cooked meals. Roasts, stews and braised dishes, as in most country districts, were more popular than grills or fried food. Traditional boaters were keen amateur sportsmen and not infrequently poachers, adept with snare, dog and gun in many canalside coverts. This brought an interesting variety to the pot, from young rabbits to hare, partridge and pheasant. Fishing from the boat is allowed on most canals but not the setting of night lines. Eels in season, mainly stewed, were popular at one period and most canal folk kept a pronged spear or harpoon for catching them.

Perhaps the favourite meal of the canal dweller is the 'pail dinner'. This is ideal when cooked for a large family in a confined space, earning top marks for home economy. The normal routine is to stand a large can or seven pound jam jar in the bottom of a dinner pail. The can is then filled with layers of sliced turnips, bacon hocks, rabbit joints, carrots and parsnips. Both pail and can are filled with water which is brought gently to the boil. A thick suet crust is then made, in the form of a lid fitting across the top of the pail, while the meat is simmering. Peeled potatoes and extra vegetables are laid on top of the pastry, a further lid or layer of suet crust being applied to aid the process of steaming. A final touch is to peel a few apples and tie them in a cloth bag with a pinch of spice or nutmeg. These are laid above the final lid, the whole being left to cook over a low heat for about two hours. When ready, a three-course meal for a large family may be taken from the same pail: soup made from the broth or gravy, followed by meat and vegetables with suet pastry, rounded off with a pudding of stewed fruit.

Pot pies are also favourites of long standing, these being cooked on the stove in a heavy iron saucepan. They are rather like a meat stew, covered, when the meat is almost ready, by a layer of suet pastry, the latter serving more as a dumpling than a traditional piecrust. Bag puddings, both sweet and savoury, are an old standby, being suet puddings made in a flour-lined bag rather than a basin. The most popular of these resemble the old English steak and kidney pudding, filled with either steak and kidney, steak and mushrooms or steak and chopped onions. The cloth bag, suspended in a saucepan of boiling water, is tied to the wooden handle of a pudding spoon fitted across the top of the pan.

The arts and customs of the canal folk developed with the ascendancy of family boating, continuing in vigour and popularity into the era of nationalisation. Yet to understand the folk culture of the canal dwellers it is also necessary to know something of their work and background, to understand them for their own sakes.

Canal scene

Chapter 2 The Owner-Boaters

Boater on the Staffordshire and Worcestershire Canal

The life of the average owner-boater, a breed now almost extinct, was one of great toughness and rigour. During later years they were mainly employed on the Grand Union and Oxford Canals, conveying coal to paper mills and power houses. The majority of 'number ones' worked in the south-east Midlands, to and from the west Midland coalfields. Although there were a few on all waterways, they represented only a small fraction of those in the abovementioned area. From the early 1930s they were under great competitive pressure from large haulage firms, especially the newly formed Grand Union Canal Company which operated its own fleet and could afford to undercut smaller traders. Competition was slightly less severe on the Oxford and Coventry Canals where there were opportunities for return loading, and some of the boaters supplied loads to small concerns, landing a ton or two at different wharves, in a trade for which the larger firms could not be bothered to tender. At such country wharves as Fenny Compton, house coal and builders' materials were trans-shipped to road vehicles for distribution to local villages.

Until well into the thirties most 'number ones' worked with horses, which remained until after the Second World War on the Oxford Canal. Work with a horse boat began at five in the morning and continued for a six- or seven-day week with stoppages only for delays in unloading, severe freezing when even icebreakers could not get through and, during the war, enemy action. The average daily journey depended on the number of locks but was about 26 miles, moving at about two miles an hour through a single pound or level. Ice was the hazard most greatly feared as canals, being still waters, froze more quickly and more deeply than rivers. Not only was great expense and loss of business involved, but also the likelihood of damage to hulls. Despite the work of the canal companies' icebreakers it was not unusual for boats to be icebound for several days, during which time families had to be fed, leaving small operators badly out of pocket.

The routine of the working day continued almost non-stop until eight or nine in the evening, the horse being lodged in canalside stables which were roughly two hours' journey apart, often at an inn or near an important flight of locks. To make deliveries, which might involve catching an early tunnel tug, a start was sometimes made before three in the morning, the horse fed, groomed and harnessed by the light of lanterns. To keep a working horse in good condition it was necessary to groom it thoroughly at both ends of the day. Boats worked over the Grand Union Canal mainly in pairs, but over the Oxford Canal as singles. The return journey with empty boats took about half the time and it was by no means unusual for a horse to tow either one or two boats a distance of 40–50 miles a day.

Canalside inn at Wolverley on the Staffordshire and Worcestershire Canal

For running a load of coal from a colliery wharf to an industrial site the boater received between £20 and £25 during the mid-1930s. Wife and family did their bit for pocket money, but where an extra hand was required he would have to be paid £1 a trip and all found. Other charges were paid to skippers of tunnel tugs; and there were stabling rents, canal tolls and fees to blacksmith and harness maker. An average tunnel fee would be 50*p* per pair loaded and 25*p* empty. On the credit side there were no rates or ground rents, coal was used from the cargo and fishing was free. The life was hard but healthy although, until the introduction of special schools, there was little incentive to education or self-improvement. Though many boaters were illiterate some managed to teach themselves to read, by studying the letters on coal wagons running over nearby railway lines; long stretches of the Grand Union Canal, for instance, ran parallel with the former LMS (ex-LNWR) main line.

During the late twenties and early thirties a pair of horse boats would cost between £450 and £500, depending on their standard of finish. This was a considerable sum for a young man in those days, especially if he was one of a large family finding it difficult to clear daily expenses. While some began life on the family boat assisting their fathers, the more fortunate would be given charge of an extra boat or pair, of which they would be the skippers-in-charge. Others worked on fly boats or found jobs in boatyards. After saving enough for a deposit the future 'number one' would order his own boat and pay instalments after each trip whenever he passed near the boatyard.

Power boats, whether steam or propelled by an internal combustion engine, were far more expensive than horse boats, which was why so many owner-boaters kept their horses long after the larger haulage firms had stopped using them. The first power boats owned by small traders were either secondhand or converted horse boats; some were rather the worse for wear. Conversion of a horse boat would cost £150. When, however, it was proved that power boats were both quicker and cheaper, earning more money in a shorter time and without incurring the costs of tunnel tugs, stabling or shoeing, there was a sudden rush to mechanise. This banished horses from most parts of the Grand Union

The Bratch, Shropshire and Worcestershire Canal. A rare type of three rise lock in which the centre gates are only a few feet apart

Canal within a space of five years. By the autumn of 1936 tunnel tugs at Braunston and Blisworth had to be withdrawn for lack of custom.

Shorter journey times and more efficient service also meant that fewer boats were needed, making competition even more severe than in horse days. However, the Oxford Canal and the Birmingham Navigations continued to be worked by horses; their narrow locks, wide enough for only one boat at a time, encouraged single boating and horse or mule working as a more economical proposition. Joe Skinner was one of the last 'number ones' on the Oxford Canal, remaining faithful to horse or mule towing until his retirement in 1959. Although a few small traders still remain, owning one or two boats for short hauls, most of the traditional families disappeared by the mid-sixties. Even in the most prosperous days of boating there were seldom more than 250 owner-boaters on the canals at any time.

Chapter 3 The Canal Boat

One of the most attractive features of the inland waterways is the traditional canal craft or narrow boat. In theory this may be worked over any part of the system from the home counties to the Welsh borders and the network of canals crossing the Pennine range. Specially designed to negotiate the low bridges and narrow lock pounds found in most areas, it is unique, unlike boats or barges in any other part of the world. Though mainly confined to inland canals narrow boats not infrequently penetrate London Docks and, even though unseaworthy in rough conditions, make short voyages over tidal reaches of Thames, Trent, Severn and other rivers. On tidal reaches with plenty of leeway it was once fairly common to see narrow boats lashed side by side (breasted up) in pairs or threes being towed by a single tug.

In the London area and home counties the narrow boat is frequently known as a 'monkey boat'. The name also spread to the Midlands and is thought to refer to a canal trader named Thomas Monk, born in Tipton, who helped to popularise the prototype during the early decades of the last century. On the Severn Navigations and in the west of England similar craft are called 'long boats'. Basic design and proportions of the narrow boat have changed very little for at least a century and a half, although in recent years British Waterways experimented with all-steel, bluff-ended craft with labour-saving hatches of fibreglass.

The trim elegant lines of the original narrow boat reflect the taste of the Georgian era; they have parallels in domestic architecture, cabinet making and the design of horsedrawn

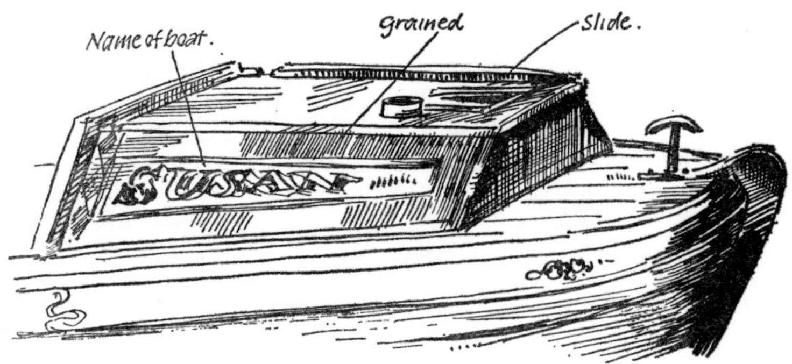

Fore cabin

vehicles. Craftsmanship of this period was arguably at its most attractive, not merely in luxuries created for the rich but in simple, practical things of daily use ranging from kitchen furniture to harvest wagons. Scholarly and pedantic designers may have been in thrall to a 'classical' heritage but even small craftsmen were affected by their example and something of higher theories filtered through to builder, mason and joiner. The basic grammar of line, proportion and harmony survived arguments over Roman or Greek orders and, when allied to needs of utility, rewarded the observer with a unique aesthetic experience. Nowhere are these characteristics more deeply sensed than in the design and workmanship of canal construction, whether buildings, engineering works or, especially, the painted narrow boats.

Boats first used on the Bridgewater Canal were mainly adapted for conveying coal from the collieries and drift mines owned by the Duke of Bridgewater to wharves in the neighbourhood of Manchester. Many of these, known as 'starvationers' because of their starved or narrow proportions, even entered underground workings and galleries which had been flooded for both drainage and navigation. These double-ended boats were ideal for their purpose. Other craft appear to have been much larger than the narrow boat; at least they were broader in the beam and are perhaps better defined as barges or wide boats. It should be remembered however that the Bridgewater Canal was constructed on more generous lines than the waterways designed by Brindley at about the same period (but not built until a few years later), including the Trent and Mersey Canal and the Staffordshire and Worcestershire Canal.

Although they were designed mainly for mineral and freight traffic it was not long before 'fly' or packet boats were introduced on most canals for the convenience of passengers, with their luggage and small packages. When roads were blocked by mud or snow for nearly half the year, travel by waterway proved much quicker and safer than venturing overland. The Duke of Bridgewater frequently travelled on his own boats; drawn by swiftly cantering horses, they were given right of way in open navigations and at bridgeholes. A sickle-shaped knife was fixed to the prow of such vessels to sever the towing lines of craft unable to make way for faster

The Duke of Bridgewater

The Duchess-Countess

traffic. The duke eventually owned a fleet of packet boats with first- and second-class cabins and coffee house refreshment for thirsty travellers. A survivor of this once-proud fleet was later turned into a houseboat and found its way to a backwater of the Shropshire Union Canal (Welsh section) where it was drawn up on the bank and occupied by an elderly recluse. It was finally left to rot. This boat was known as the *Duchess-Countess* and seems to have been typical of craft used on the Bridgewater Navigations during the eighteenth century. Its graceful curves are closely akin to the modern narrow boat and may long have inspired the builders of traditional craft as a model of all that was desirable and necessary.

Other types of boat used on the narrow canals, modified for the shorter locks of certain sections or built with smaller cabins for day trips only, are merely versions of the standard narrow boat which survived the era of horse towing to reappear as the 'butty' or rear boat of a modern working pair. The first boat of the pair is a specially designed power craft acting as tug which also provides additional cargo and cabin space. It owes much to established tenets of design but is less elegant than the horse boat, especially at the stern end, and from the late 1920s is usually of all-steel or composite construction. Composite boats, both motor boats and butties,

Working pair breasted-up (the butty has the higher cratch)

have steel sides but wooden bottoms, decking and stern cabins. From the late 1930s very few boats of all-wooden construction were built, although even steel boats follow the lines of traditional narrow craft, using less familiar materials. A popular new type of this era, which soon began to dominate the lower reaches of the Grand Union Canal, is the so-called 'town boat', designed and built in the yards of Messrs Harland and Wolff at Woolwich. Although surviving in other parts of the country it was claimed that the wooden narrow boat with horse towing was virtually extinct in the south-eastern division of the waterways shortly after the Second World War.

The butty was originally worked as a horse boat, often in identical pairs, towed either by one or two horses, two mules or a mule and a horse in tandem. Two horses in tandem were a rare sight. Worked as singles the butties would be hauled by a single horse or mule or two donkeys.

The name 'butty' originated in the mining districts of the north-east and Midlands, denoting either an old comrade or member of a working party employed on a contract basis. The terms 'butty pal', 'butty collier' or butty gang' were once frequently used between Tyne and Trent. The butty boat, either steel or wood, is generally considered the flagship or main living boat of a working pair. It often receives slightly more care and attention from the boaters concerned, being more likely to display fine examples of traditional painting than its more modern counterpart.

Front ends in profile. Butty (*top*) and motorboat

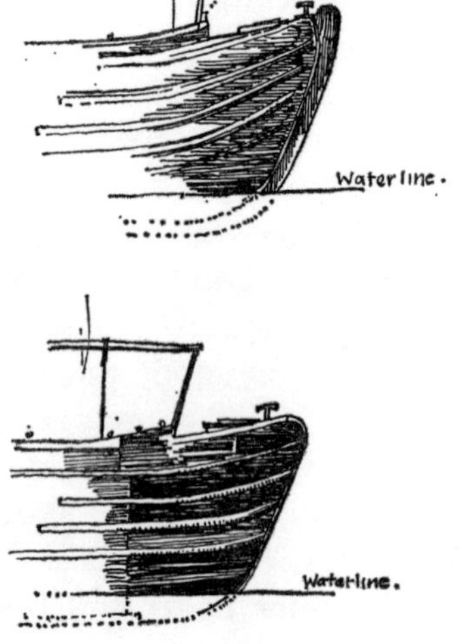

A limited number of steam-powered canal boats worked over most inland waterways from the 1860s to the 1920s. These had either wooden or steel hulls and were smaller than the average narrow boat with more space devoted to the engine and boiler than was considered economical. Perhaps the finest were those operated by Fellows, Morton and Clayton and kept in immaculate condition with carpets on the engine room floor. Protective curtains prevented the engines from being dirtied by smuts and coal dust. Most of the steamers were converted to diesel power after 1920, acquiring extra cargo and living space through a reduction in engine size, elimination of boiler space and reduced fuel storage. Steamers were usually 'fly' boats operated by an all-male crew.

Stern ends in profile. Motorboat (*top*) and butty

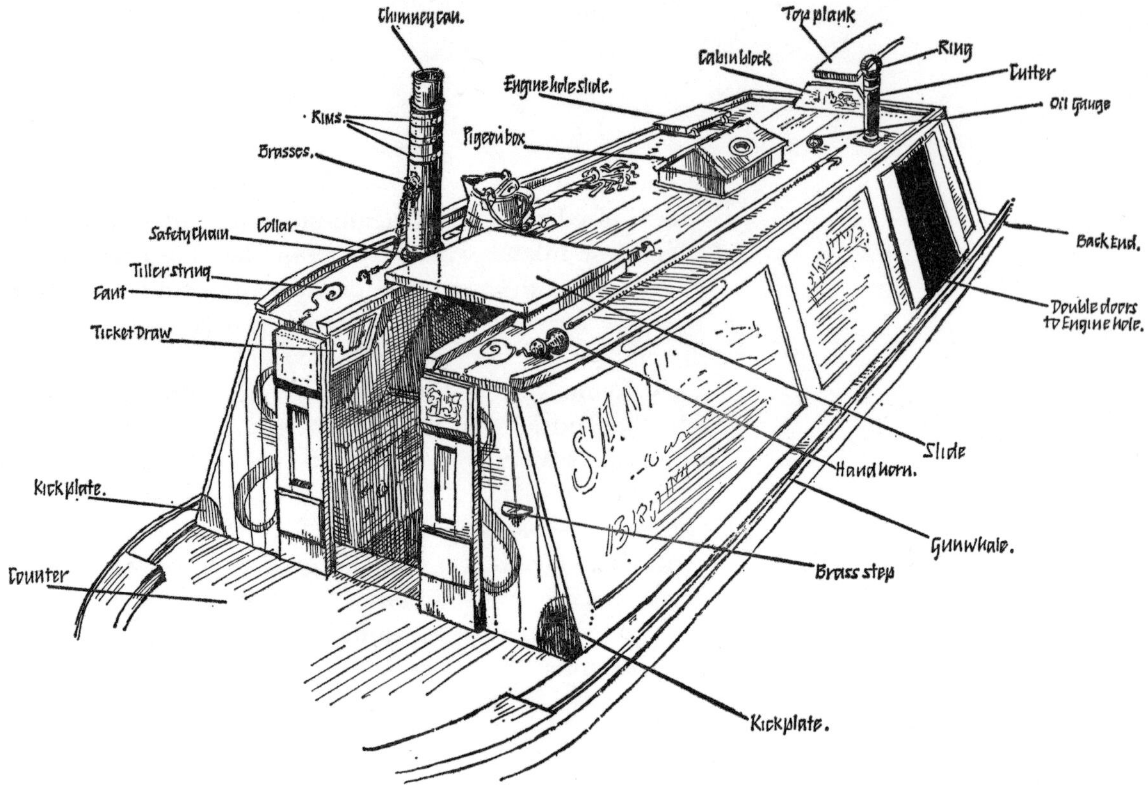

Chimney can.
Top plank
Ring
Cabin block
Cutter
Engine hole slide.
Oil Gauge
Rims.
Pigeon box
Brasses.
Back End.
Collar
Safety chain
Tiller string
Cant
Double doors to Engine hole.
Ticket Draw
Slide
Hand horn.
Kickplate.
Gunwhale.
Brass step
Counter
Kickplate.

Stern end of motorboat

Spare plank.
Bulls eye
Top plank.
Safety chain.
Cabin block.
Cant.
Drip-off
Cant
Cabin Strings.
Top Strip.
Hook.
Guard.
Shackle

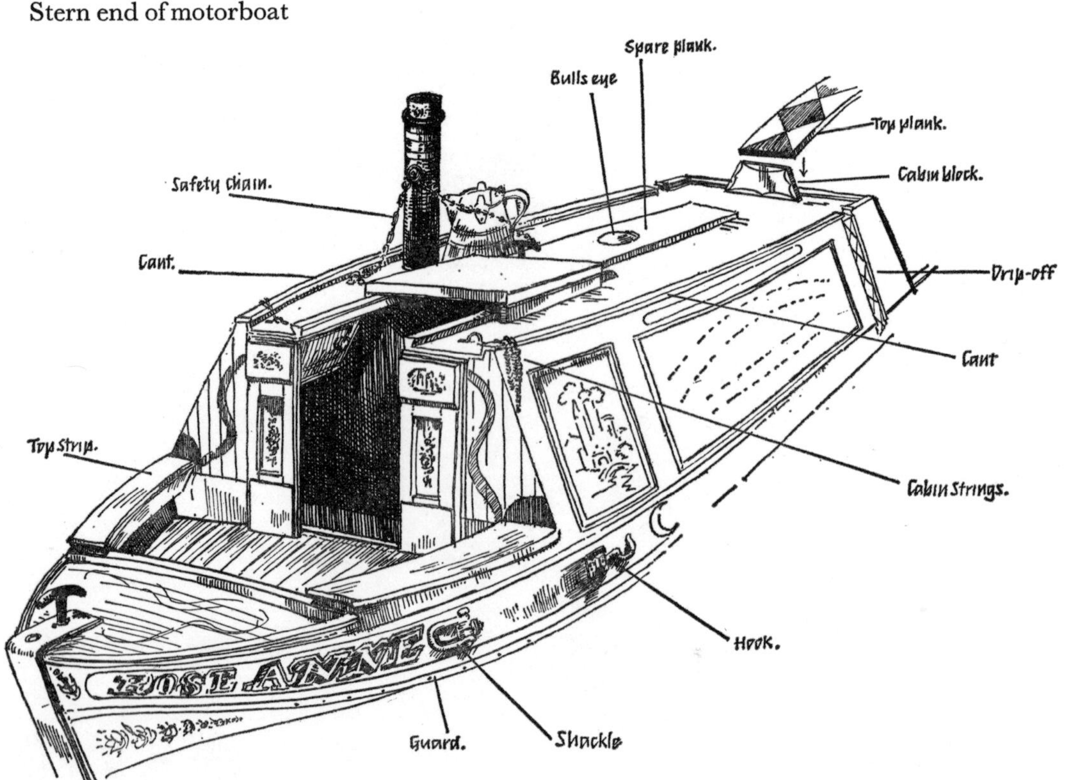

Stern end of butty

Construction of the butty boat

The traditional wooden butty, of which type many were still in use until the 1950s, was mainly constructed of oak and elm with planking laid edge to edge in 'carvel' style. Carvel style, as opposed to 'clinker' build with overlapping planks, is thought to have derived from the shipbuilding techniques of the Mediterranean and the caravel or light sailing ship of this area which existed before the Roman empire. Clinker build, in which upper planks were laid above lower planks and fixed with clinched nails, was a technique of northern waters, rarely if ever used for canal craft or river barges.

During construction the timbers of a wooden boat were supported several feet above the ground on a wooden framework. This appeared to be roughly the same shape as the flat-bottomed hull but slightly broader in the beam.

Oak was used for the hull or main bodywork, the bottom was usually of fine quality elm. Oak timbers above and below the waterline were dry or wet according to cargo weight and were therefore treated with various waterproof coatings. When fully loaded the gunwale of the narrow boat

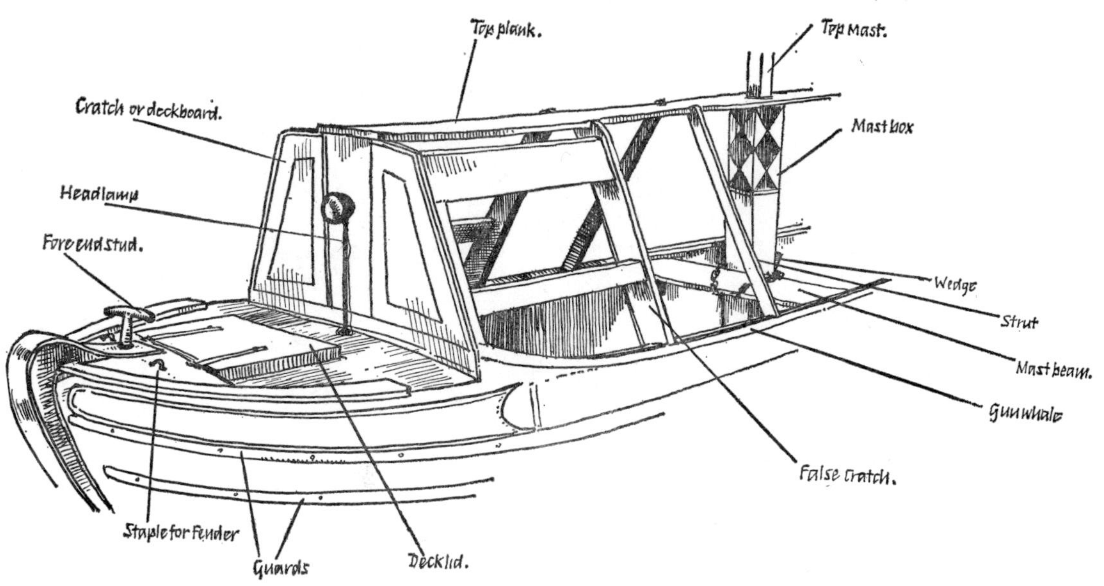

Fore end of butty showing construction of cratch

was only a few inches above water level so that the upper parts were frequently splashed or saturated if not submerged, especially when passing through locks. The flat elm bottom on the other hand was left untreated to absorb as much water as possible. Elm bottoms exposed in this way merely hardened and are known to have lasted for many years. When allowed to dry out however, through contact with light and air, they soon began to crumble.

The first canal boats with elm bottoms were constructed with longitudinal planks known as 'long bottoms'. They were made without a keelson and were spiked to transverse ribs or timbers of seasoned oak. In more recent years however there has always been a fairly deep keelson of oak or pitch pine, and elm planks of transverse pattern were reinforced with longitudinal strakes and bolted to iron or steel supports which served as connections between oak and elm. Oak planks were often shaped and strengthened in specially designed steam chests.

Stern of butty showing depth of hull empty

Tillers of motorboat (nearside) and butty

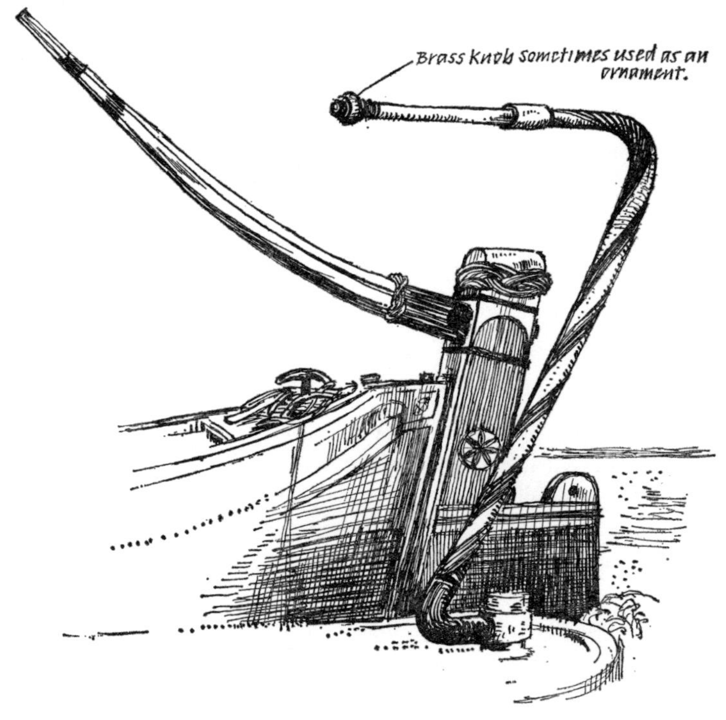

Once the hull was completed the sides were daubed with a protective mixture of 'chalico'; cowhair, horse dung and Stockholm tar boiled together. No effective substitute was found for these ingredients, dung being frequently provided by canalside stables where boaters left their horses overnight or between trips.*

After the application of chalico the inner surface of the hull was covered with layers of stiff brown paper or strips of light felt, which in turn disappeared under thin oak planks or 'shearings'. Seams were caulked with pitch and oakum, the whole outer surface being dressed with hot tar.

* Horses were stabled compulsorily and were prevented from being turned loose for grazing, according to byelaws.

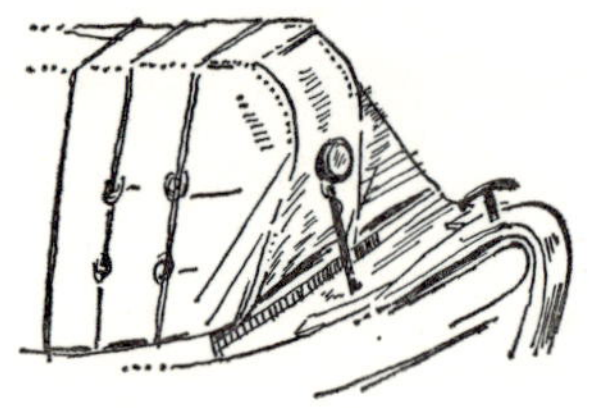

Bulk from front end

As a secondary stage work was concentrated on design and construction of cabins, masts and decking. The whole structure of the boat was strengthened at various intervals by detachable cross planks known as thwarts or 'stretchers'. These fitted into lining pieces or brackets slightly lower than the gunwales. Uprights or stands supporting a centre gangway of top planks appeared at intervals in the cargo space, the whole completed by top planks fixed to stands and resting at one end on the stern cabin (or a block above the roof of the cabin) and, at the other end, on a triangular front board or 'cratch'. A false decking was then laid, covering the floor of cargo space and cabin, its planking flush with the keelson. Rudder and rudder post, known collectively as the 'elum', were shipped next and the towing or box mast stepped. The foot of the mast fitted into the keelson as a mortice and tenon joint. Main structural features of decking and living quarters completed, the boat was then prepared for painting and rigged with protective covers.

Dimensions of the traditional wooden narrow boat are 70–72 ft. long with a 7 ft. beam and empty draught of 8 in. Carrying capacity on a canal reasonably free from silting is up to 25 tons.

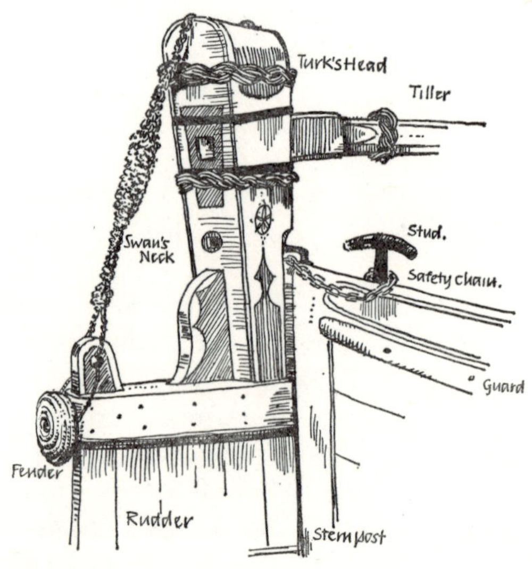

The elum

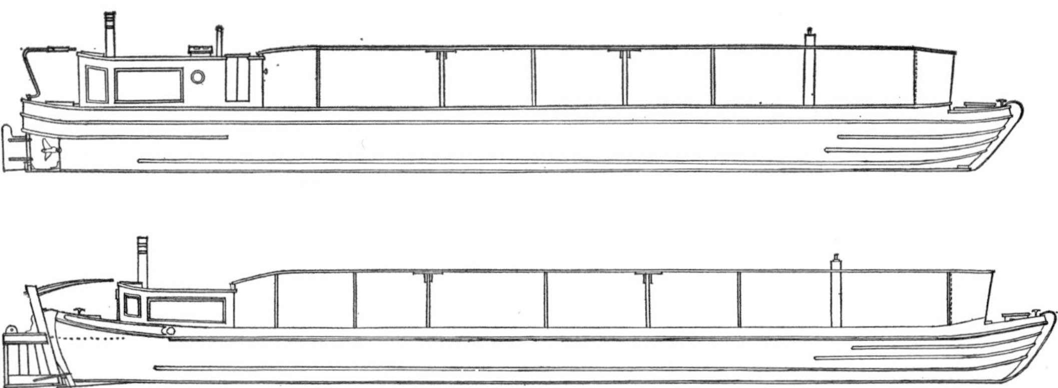

Narrow boats in profile. Motorboat (*top*) and butty

Types of narrow boat

Most narrow boats were built to order so they were almost but not quite identical. They were mainly constructed in canalside boatyards in different parts of the Midlands, home counties and industrial north. Perhaps the finest and most characteristic were built in the south Midlands, especially in the Braunston yards of Messrs Nurser Brothers. They were recognisable products, not only of their builders and designers, but for certain details specified by future owners. The so-called 'Fellows boat', used in large numbers by the carrying firm of Fellows, Morton and Clayton Limited, had a sleeker line than most of its contemporaries, with limited freeboard when loaded, high towing masts, stands, cratch and blocks and well-raked at bow and stern. The stern cabin of a Fellows boat was of medium height above water level, with regular side panels on the tumblehome. A tapered rubbing band and name space rose with graceful upward curves towards stern post and rudder. The cratch or front board on this type was made to lean well forward.

Fore ends of typical narrow boats. (*Left to right*) Star class, Admiral class-BW, All-steel butty, Barlow B, Runcorn Bt.

The 'Barlow boat', favoured by the Birmingham firm of coal factors and carrying agents of that name, was of average height but without distinctive side panels, its stern cabin having flush sides. Masts and stands were slightly taller than average with high slack or wash boards placed forward of the stern cabin so as to increase the quantity of loose coal that could be carried. Because stands were fairly high the final section of the top planks frequently curved down to a deep block on the fore part of the stern cabin roof. Many of the Nurser-designed boats (most Barlow boats were in this category) had a removable cratch or front board that was noted for its colourful decoration.

Boats from the yards of Messrs Walkers Limited of Rickmansworth, on the Grand Union Canal, had larger, more generous proportions than the average craft and worked with difficulty through certain sections of the Trent and Mersey Canal or similar waterways, being for that reason mainly confined to areas south of Birmingham. Cabin sides were higher and straighter, lacking the inward slope or tumblehome typical of Midland craft. Other features of Walker-built narrow boats included a long, inward curving stern or afterdeck and deeply recessed side panels along the near-upright sides of the superstructure. On a broad canal or with plenty of leeway, many boaters claimed that Walker boats were a joy to handle. Most of them had much higher sides than the Nurser boats even when fully loaded. The Walker boat was bluffer in general appearance with less rake at stem and stern than most canal craft.

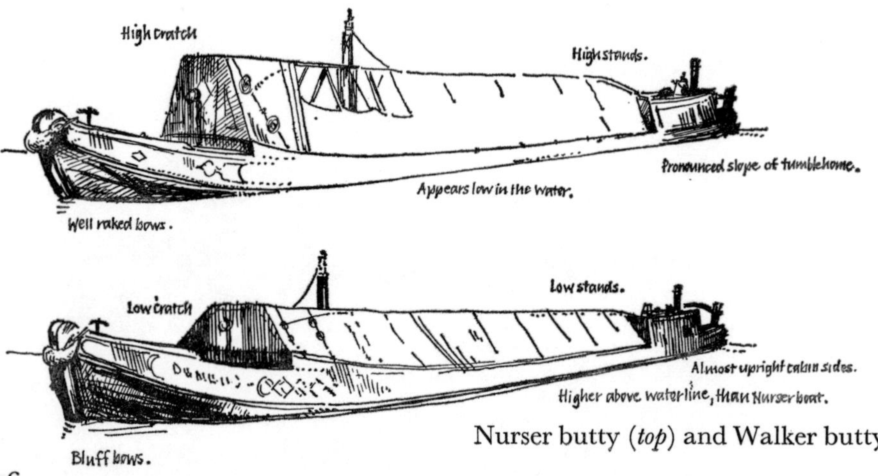

Nurser butty (*top*) and Walker butty

The size of boats depended on cargoes handled and routes travelled. Their width and length were determined by the size of the smallest lock through which they were expected to work. With a greater regional variety of locks and widths of canal in mind, boats built in northern and north Midlands yards tended to be more varied than craft operating south of Birmingham. Such yards as Taylors of Chester tended to turn out smaller boats than southern builders, while Yarwoods of Northwich built types similar to Walker boats.

The so-called 'Runcorn boats', owned by the Runcorn Company, were massive in both appearance and dimensions, with barrel-shaped holds and almost vertical stern and stem posts. They were more like barges than narrow boats, decorated with scrollwork rather than traditional roses and castles. Capacity was about five tons more than the average narrow boat. Originally horse-drawn, a large number were converted into power boats in about 1913 with a propeller shaft fitted through the stern post and false cheeks, or side pieces, attached to the afterdeck to form a more balanced counter stern.

About 1937 a large fleet of all-steel and composite boats was constructed for the Grand Union Canal Company. These resembled the Walker or 'Ricky' (Rickmansworth) boats in appearance and handling qualities, far more than other types. The new fleet was divided between smaller 'Star' class boats, named after the heavenly bodies, and the larger 'Town' class. Capacity was identical but 'Town' boats were frequently used on tidal waters and given extra freeboard with substantial build to prevent them shipping wash from larger vessels.

The short-lived 'Royalty' class, to be named after kings and queens, but of which only six were built, were slightly larger than 'Town' boats. One of them, originally named *Victoria* but renamed *Linda*, still survives in the Birmingham district.

The latest development was the 'River' class butty, often towed by the 'Admiral' class tug or power boat. These were designed for British Waterways and introduced about 1958. They were constructed with blunt, vertical ends from welded light gauge steel sheets. The butty had fibreglass hatches in place of canvas or tarpaulin covers.

As a general rule faster boats for 'fly' or packet services were slightly longer and narrower than those for minerals and general cargo. With more tapering lines they were, in designers' idiom, 'fast shapes'. The wooden-hulled Shropshire fly boats ('Shroppie flies') working between Liverpool and Birmingham were only 6 ft. wide and 2 ft. deep. Many of this type, bringing perishable goods from Liverpool docks to the Midlands, were drawn by cantering horses worked in tandem and changed every few miles.

The day boats of the Birmingham Navigations were shorter and far less elegant than family boats in bulk and proportions, sometimes being double-ended since it was possible to hang their rudders at each end to avoid turning in confined spaces. Some of the day boats operated by 'Joey boaters' on short trips lacked a stern cabin or even shelter. These were frequently known as 'rubbish boats' and used on short hauls for the disposal of factory waste. Most later craft of this type however had a small cabin for cooking and eating, but not for sleeping. Large day boats working between Cannock and Wolverhampton, known as 'Ampton boats' were confined to an area of canal without locks and measured up to 80 ft. in length.

It is widely recognised that family boats in the hands of responsible boaters are usually those kept in the best condition and up to the highest general standards of smartness and decoration. Day boats are sometimes in the hands of different crews for each journey and are often neat and well cared for while lacking the finishing touches of the best family boats. 'Rodney boats' are usually knocked to pieces by a drunken, irresponsible crew with no real interest in either their work or reputation on the waterways.

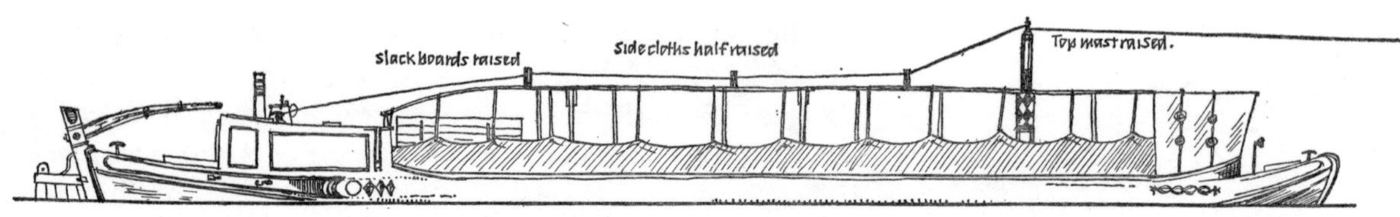

Butty using running blocks for towing

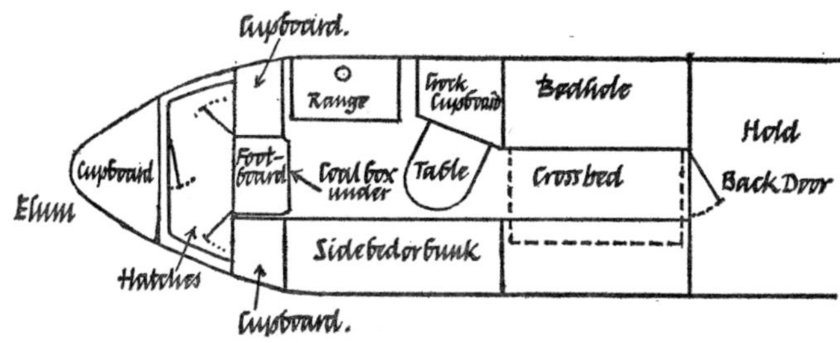

Plan of stern cabin of butty

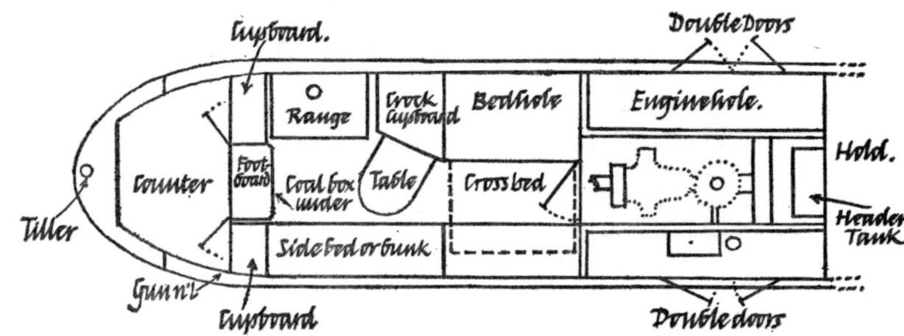

Plan of stern cabin of motorboat

Description of a typical narrow boat

The bow or stem of the average narrow boat is more or less bluff, varying according to locality and design. The rake of the front end or stem post is not less than 1 ft. 8 in. and rarely more than 2 ft. 6 in.

A short decked area extends back from the stem post to the cargo space, seldom more than 5 ft. 6 in. to 5 ft. 8 in. long. This can be either a small fore cabin, suitable as a bedroom, or a storage place for spare fenders and similar gear. A square hatchway covered by a slide or hinged deck lid is normally set in the centre of the sloping foredeck. The hinges of the lid are fixed to the triangular forward section of the prow, opening towards the stem post. Between the deck and the stem post is a T-shaped bar with a curved top fixed through the stem iron, known as the 'fore end stud' or mooring stud, used for towing and mooring purposes. On the opposite side of the deck lid most craft carry a navigation lamp. This was formerly sheathed in copper or richly painted with floral motifs but from the 1930s was more likely to be an electric side lamp from a motor van. Many early butties, of a type rarely seen after the 1950s, had enlarged fore cabins with raised sides for extra headroom; these side boards were at least a foot above the gunwales. Such boards were often painted with the boat's name.

The foredeck terminates in a near-upright cratch or triangular structure fixed above the main entrance to the forecabin from the cargo space. This, either decorated in elaborate style or covered by tarpaulins, is sometimes fitted with a useless but decorative object known as a 'bulk'. The bulk has a rotund or bulbous contour; it is made of taut canvas on a flexible framework and stuffed with hay or straw. The cratch itself may be designed to tilt slightly forward, the upper line of the gunwale also curving upwards at this point as though to repeat even more generous curves between cratch and stem post.

The cratch on smaller boats is frequently known as the deck or front board. Its main function is to support the foremost top plank of a gangway between fore and stern cabins. A structure of planks and struts a few feet farther back is known as the 'false cratch'. The rest of the top planks abaft the false cratch are supported by upright stands, the box mast and a number of inward-leaning struts, the final top plank resting on the stern cabin roof.

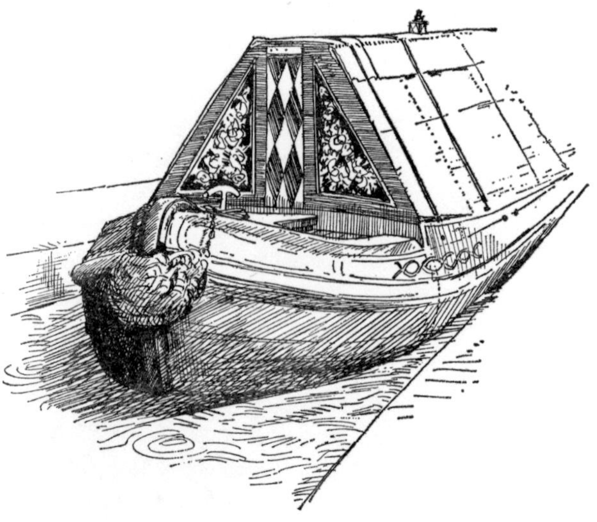

Fore end of butty showing decorated cratch

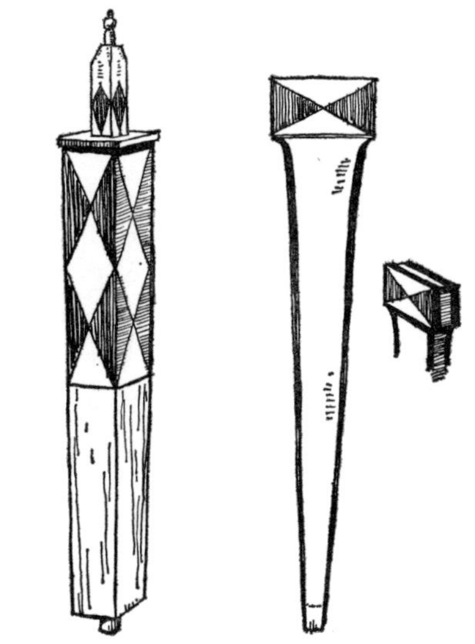

Box mast (*left*) and stand

The box mast, foremast or towing post is the first important vertical feature in the cargo space. It occupies a central position, and is secured at its base to the keelson. The upper part is telescopic and may be raised or depressed above or below the level of the top planks. Special pulley gear fitted to the upper part of the mast is used when the butty is towed with running blocks: that is, when the towing rope is fixed to a rear stud and guided through blocks over the pulley of the mast. The lower part of the box mast, also known as the mastbox, is secured at the front to a timber thwart or 'mast beam', some masts being wedged and chained in position. When a boat is fully loaded the top mast is raised to full extent, to clear the towing line and prevent it fouling the cargo. Day boats had plain solid masts without the telescopic section.

Two other verticals, known as 'stands', are spaced between box mast and stern cabin. They rest in sockets on the false deck but are also attached to cross beams. Stands are attenuated wedges, much narrower at the base than the top, fairly narrow but presenting a broader shape fore and aft. The top of each stand forms a rectangular block designed as a support for top planks. Painted wooden struts, up to five a side, form a framework for the protective covers.

Side cloths for the protection of cargoes are fixed to the gunwales in rolls and may be drawn up by cords passed over the top planks. Four top cloths of heavy duty canvas may be let down from above. When the boat is fully rigged a narrow strip of lighter canvas, mainly for show, is also let down from the top planks. Semi-permanent covers at the fore end between cratch and false cratch are secured by narrow white cords or 'strings', the ends of which are finished in ornamental knots and coils.

There are several variations of rigging to cover the hold, depending on the type of cargo carried. It is thought unnecessary to draw the side cloths right to the top unless a perishable cargo is carried. With other loads the cloths are half drawn up to prevent water washing in at the sides. Stone and pile boats are left fully open, in which case stands are removed and top planks rest on cross beams, forming a gangway slightly above the level of the cargo space. The space between cratch and false cratch is nearly always covered with tarpaulins except in the rare case of an open load. A fully rigged boat complete with side and top cloths resembles a long floating tent.

The stern end of the top plank is bent down to the cabin roof where it frequently rests on a painted wooden section known as a cabin block. This varies in height according to the type of craft but is larger on a butty than a power boat. Three separate running blocks appear at intervals along the top planks to guide the towing rope or 'snubber' which is also passed over a pulley of the box mast as previously described. At the extreme stern end the snubber is attached to a cabin stud near the cockpit slide. Most running blocks are round-topped and chamfered, having sheaves or apertures to guide the snubber.

Main living quarters on narrow boats are in the stern cabin at the rear of the cargo space. This measures between 8 and 10 ft. in length with 7 ft. maximum width and headroom variable between 5 ft. and 5 ft. 6 in. There are doors on opposite sides of the cabin communicating with both steerage and cargo space. In the case of the butty the cargo entrance is known as the back door, a feature often missing on the power boat. The sides of the cabin have a marked inward pitch or tumblehome above the gunwale and an almost flat roof that rises slightly towards the stern. The angle of the tumblehome depends mainly on the general style and capacity of the narrow boat but it is steeper on the power boat than the butty.

A stovepipe from the solid fuel range rises about three feet above the cabin roof of the butty. The top of it might be bound with three brass bands known as 'rims', often missing on boats of northern origin. The pipe is fixed on the left of the cockpit slide, looking forward, at the stern end of the cabin. It is secured to the roof by a brass safety chain. In some cases the cabin chimney has an extension, a painted (hollow) tin can for extra height and better draughting. The top of the cabin is surrounded by a bevelled strip of wood, or 'cant', with drainage slots on both sides of the fore end letting on to a water drip or groove down the sloping sides of the cabin.

A square cockpit at the stern end of the cabin offers partial protection for steering in cold weather, the helmsman or woman standing on a cross plank above the coal box, the latter also forming a step down into the cabin. The stern entrance to cabin and cockpit has double doors, and the top aperture may be covered by a painted slide.

Beyond the cockpit at the stern end is a small area of well-deck known as 'hatches', protected at rear and sides by inward-curving sections of wood each trimmed with a flat highly scrubbed top strip. A small stern deck tapers inwards and curves slightly upwards abaft the hatches to meet the stern post. A storage locker is constructed under the stern deck with main access from the cockpit. A stern or back stud rises above deck level immediately before the stern post.

The 'elum' rudder post or ram's head is attached to the stern post, tilting backwards at an angle of 75 degrees. The tiller curves down from the ram's head to the cockpit in an elegant sweep, but is reversed or inverted out of harm's way when the boat moors for the night.

Although the power or 'motor' boat is in many ways similar to the butty it differs slightly at the stern end, which tends to be of a rounded or counter shape lifting clear of the water above the single driving screw and shaft. The deck of the power boat is frequently known as the 'counter'. The tiller of a motor boat is also less elegant than that of a butty or horse boat, being a tubular Z-shape, often with a brass rod or extension. While the cabin area of the power boat seems externally much longer than that of the butty this is mainly to accommodate engine and fuel tank; actual living space may in some cases be slightly smaller than on the older type of craft. Double doors on both sides of the boat communicate directly with the engine space or 'hole', while a further door (equivalent to the back door on a butty) provides access to the engine from the living quarters.

The cabin roof of a power boat is slightly more cluttered with structures than the roof of a butty. In addition to the stovepipe there are either one or two exhaust pipes. The top of each pipe usually has an upright metal ring or 'cutter' across the aperture. Its purpose (it is sometimes known as a 'tunnel cutter') is to break up fumes and smoke, especially in low tunnels and bridgeholes, and to keep soot and grit from falling down the chimney from a tunnel roof. The actual exhaust pipe varies in length, size and position. When situated on the side of a boat, where it is likely to be knocked by overhanging foliage, it is short and squat. The exhaust pipe of a twin cylinder engine is tall and narrow; that of a single cylinder is much wider and shorter. A spare exhaust pipe and ring or cutter are frequently carried, fixed to an outside bracket of the forward bulkhead. Other objects on the power boat's cabin roof include an engine hole slide to the left and a hatchway cover, with hinged flaps and brass rimmed ports, known as the 'pigeon box'. The latter brings light and air to the engine hole, frequently having replaced an inverted box-shape or 'lift off hatch' later associated with wooden boats only. A brass-mounted hand horn stands on the right of the cockpit slide. Controls such as the 'speed wheel' (throttle) and clutch project at the ends of steel rods from under the cabin slide.

Strakes at bow and stern of most narrow boats follow the curves of the hull, emphasising their elegant lines. The uppermost of these are known as 'guards'. Between the upper guard and gunwale at the stern cabin end are hooks and shackles used in breasting up a pair of boats when passing through double locks or in river navigation. The fore end of the butty sometimes has a pattern of twisted metal on either side of the hull below the cratch. Known as 'snakes', these are used both as protective barriers and decorations. Snakes have also been known to appear, but less frequently, at the stern end of a butty.

An interesting feature of the building of narrow boats is the casual way they were designed, especially the wooden boats. Rule of thumb methods amounted almost to a tradition on the early canals, following the maxim that 'if a thing looks right it is right'. Complex plans and blueprints were almost unknown, although models were sometimes made of new or unusual types, often for special orders. Most yards however kept roughly bound books or folders in which main dimensions were sketched and recorded.

Interior fittings of the narrow boat

The furniture of a typical narrow boat is made to fit into a small space or fold away as part of the interior structure. Stools nest together; the table is a flap or panel let down from the front of the crock cupboard. Bunks are made up on the tops of lockers which in daytime serve as benches. Even the the lid of the coal box, kept near the door, is used as a step down from cockpit to cabin.

Cupboards, drawers and lockers are the main storage places, with ticket drawer, windlass hole and soap hole near the cabin entrance. There is also limited storage space under

Cabin of butty looking towards the stern

the stern deck. The ticket drawer, on the left from the stern end, is just beyond the double doors within the cockpit area. It contains lock passes which may be reached by the helmsman without his leaving the tiller. The windlass hole is a round open compartment, much lower than the ticket drawer, on the opposite side of the stern cabin. This is reserved for the windlass and spare windlass used in opening the paddles of lock gates. A member of the family or crew, known as a 'lock wheeler', usually cycles along the towing path to open gates well in advance. The soap hole explains itself and is a small aperture directly beneath the ticket drawer. Soap is kept near the cockpit entrance as this is the working end of the boat and most of the washing is done on the cabin roof or small stern deck. Other cleaning materials, such as metal polish, rags and brushes, are kept in a semicircular drawer, also near the cabin doors, known as a 'monkey box' or 'monkey hole'.

On the left of the entrance doors the most impressive feature is the combined cooking and heating range, of patent design and burning solid fuel, usually small coal but sometimes coke. It is an oblong or box-shaped object of cast iron with a protective rail along the top and front. The elaborately hinged oven section in most cases is on the left of the heating stove. Pots and pans are boiled on the top of the stove, and there is nearly always a kettle boiling for fresh tea. Part of the stove chimney or pipe is inside the cabin, tilted forward at an angle of 60 degrees to match the inward-sloping walls, this section being partly sheathed in brass or copper and serving as a movable damper. One or two brass rails directly above the range are used for drying clothes and dish cloths.

Opposite the range is a bench bunk, under which may be found a clothes locker or drawers. This is usually a child's bunk, smaller than the folding or cross bunk at the head of the cabin, which lets down from a section of the wall known as the 'bed hole' or 'bed hole cupboard' at right angles to the bench bunk. Cupboards are usually located above the bed hole and drawers below.

Space directly above and beside the stove is used for hanging pans, jugs, plates and horse brasses. Canal folk were among the first to appreciate the decorative effect of

Narrow boat cabin looking forward

horse brasses, which have since found their way into perhaps too many homes. Most ledges and shelves are trimmed with crochet work, produced by the womenfolk on winter evenings, and the side of the crock cupboard next to the stove is covered with rows of plates and dishes.

The front of the crock cupboard is at an angle of 15 degrees to the cabin side walls. Its upper part, concealed by a hinged flap with an inlaid centre panel, is painted with traditional landscapes, often including the castle motif. Round the top and sides of the centre panel all flat surfaces are decorated with small swags of roses or other floral patterns. A brass or china knob in the top lefthand corner is used for raising and lowering the flap. Two or three knobs however are by no means unusual. Once the flap is lowered, revealing the contents of the crock cupboard, the upper surface is converted into a table top. When the flap is raised any crumbs or small fragments fall into a shallow drawer beneath, designed for that purpose. Crockery is both decorative and useful, often including Staffordshire and semi-valuable Measham ware. Each crock cupboard has upper and lower shelves, with larger, more decorative pieces in the upper section. There is usually a brass bar across the front of the upper shelf, and the sides of the cupboard are festooned with crochet work. Amongst the array of crockery might be found wedding presents and souvenirs from past holidays, including sets of miniature candlesticks, tiny horseshoes and brass windlass handles. There are sometimes two or more drawers beneath the crock cupboard, with space for second best china; there is also a boot hole or cupboard.

Space is of necessity cramped, making it difficult to move about without ducking or stooping. When bunks and tables are set out movement is even further restricted, although some butties acquire extra space through having a small fore cabin in the bows beyond the cargo space, often large enough for two or three children.

Curtains divide the living cabin into halves beyond the crock cupboard, the farther part being known as the bedroom. Each set of curtains has a deep pelmet and valance, its lacework ornamented with diamond-shaped insets trimmed with crocheting and with blue ribbons or tassels along the lower borders. Framed photographs, more plates (usually lace plates with open work borders) and burnished windlass handles hang in front of the curtains, especially round and above the partition.

Although many boats of later years are fitted with electric lighting generated from the engine of the power boat, oil lamps with tall glass funnels were long prized as ornaments. These were attached to decorative brackets projecting from the sides of the crock cupboards, not unlike candle brackets on a Victorian upright piano. Shades used on bracket lamps were festooned with large bows and fringed tails of ribbon and secured with a pictorial brooch. The portrait or cameo on the brooch was usually a member of the royal family.

In some cabins there are several clocks, which serve both as ornaments and symbols of prosperity. When there is only one clock it is usually fixed on top of the cupboard above the table flap.

Floor coverings range from rush matting to gaudy rugs and squares of lino, the latter frequently in crude 'jazz age' colours. In many boats the whole floor surface is covered with fitted lino from wall to wall.

Portable items of furniture include stools, clothes boxes and coal boxes, to which some modern boaters have added a battery-operated radio and either a hand- or treadle-worked sewing machine. Fire irons are sometimes duplicated, with a set in twisted brass (polished at least once every two days) merely for show. Every item with a suitable surface is hand-painted in traditional colours and patterns, seeming to be appreciated as much for appearance as for use. Boaters are great traditionalists, regarding the correct form, design and even layout of their surroundings with superstitious concern.

Everything is decorated in one way or another, from the fuel tank of a power boat to an ordinary tea tray or sugar box. In addition to tassels, bobbles, bows and even brass knobs, some boaters fix to interior walls of cabins tiny brass bells, which jangle and clash when boats run into a lock pound or against a wharf. Every living cabin has at least one stool, painted on the outside with roses or castles, the top of the seat sometimes lifting on hinges to reveal an inner compartment. Some stools are small and suitable only for young children.

During the eighteenth and nineteenth centuries all boats carried a small drinking water barrel mounted horizontally on a still or wooden trestle. This contained freshly drawn water and was placed on the roof of the cabin. With the later introduction of taps and stand pipes at various intervals along the canalside the barrels became obsolete but, with their attractive brasswork in the form of hoops and spigots, were frequently retained as ornaments. The bung of each barrel was mounted with a large china knob. Boats on northern waterways frequently had a large water barrel with an opening near the top from which water was taken with a scoop or dipper.

In the days of horses and mules spare items of harness were often carried in the boat cabins, from which the brasses survived to recent years. These included bits, bridles and as many as three spare collars. Brass harness mountings would be stamped with the initials of either the boat owner or the firm for which the boater worked. Another colourful feature of horse days was the hand-painted metal can or 'nose bowl' used for feeding horses. This was carried on the stern deck or cabin roof when not in use.

The decoration and formality of cabin interiors extends to the exterior and the cabin roof, especially where the layout and arrangement of portable items is concerned. A large water can containing at least three gallons of fresh water is stationed on the roof beside the stove chimney, next to which might be placed a dipper or water bowl with a short handle. Smaller cans are sometimes kept inside the cabin for show and not always displayed on the roof. Outside cans are chained to the chimney or stovepipe for safety. The can is used only for drinking and culinary purposes; water for washing and cleaning is scooped out of the canal and thrown back after use. The dipper however is far more than a container and is also used for washing clothes and peeling vegetables. Some of the earlier types of can and dipper were ornamented, not only with roses and castles but also with good luck mottoes and verses.

When the dipper is not in use it is placed upside down with its handle resting on the edge of the cockpit slide. A mop, its handle patterned with spiral stripes not unlike a barber's pole or the tiller of a power boat, lies between water can and dipper. This is frequently a rag mop, twirled or 'trundled' by the boat woman over her left arm in a characteristic manner.

Odd corners of the stern cabin roof may be filled with potted plants or even a chained brass birdcage. By tradition a length of coiled rope is lodged on the righthand side of the cockpit slide. Other cords attached to the cabin roof are used for lashing the tiller when breasting up in double locks. Some boats carry an extra top plank, often used as a gangplank between stern deck and wharf, forward of the cockpit. The power boat frequently carries a boathook or 'shaft'.

Less familiar items of equipment include brass-bound or copper-sheathed masthead lamps, attached to the front board or cratch, for night work or navigating long tunnels. Some of these are now held in reserve or kept for show for most have been replaced by car or van headlamps. Oil lamps are of two main types, with a round or straight lens protecting the lamp.

A variation of the fish spear with five prongs, or an eel catching trident, may have survived on some boats from the early nineteenth century but it was little used after the turn of the century.

The typical narrow boat anchor, usually stowed in the fore cabin, is known as a 'catcher'. It is mainly used by craft venturing into rivers and tidal waters, such as the Thames at Brentford near its junction with the Grand Union Canal. A catcher is about 16 in. long with a small ring at one end and an inverted fluke at the other.

Chapter 4 Boat Painting and Decoration

Part one: The Subject

Swag of roses

Evolving tradition

The tradition of decorating family boats on the inland waterways may be traced back as far as the mid-nineteenth century. There are references to painted narrow boats in the writings of Charles Dickens, mainly in the magazine *Household Words*, dating back to the 1850s. Boaters claim that painting roses and castles goes back even further into history and is as old as the design of narrow boats themselves. It is true that early paintings and engravings of canal subjects depict boats with only a minimum of decoration, but it is possible that such craft were the packet or 'fly' boats owned by large carrying companies rather than family boats on which decorative traditions developed to full effect. Also, it would prove a task of great difficulty to reproduce the lively flourish of a narrow boat's roses and castles on the small scale of the average easel painting, much less a steel engraving or lithograph.

As with most genuine traditions the decoration of canal craft has doubtless undergone many changes, improvements and even recessions during the course of two centuries. It is certainly not as dormant as critics of folk art make believe. Yet, like the boaters themselves, it is governed by its own rules, and should not be judged against traditional painting or *avant garde* experiments.

The ancestors of the canal folk were mainly industrious, unspoiled countrymen, small farmers displaced by land enclosures, village craftsmen and skilled labourers. Given the chance such men, of all nations, attempt to improve and decorate the vehicles or tools with which they work, or the buildings and other objects by which they are surrounded. This is because traditional skills and occupations become a way of life rather than a living, and it is part of the human condition to seek creative outlets searching for symbolism and order in the seeming chaos of nature. It is no part of these chapters to probe into motives of human psychology, yet from the evidence of the past it seems clear that a need for decoration and an urge to create, in various media, have played an important role in man's evolution.

At one time it was possible that all craft were decorated by the boaters themselves. In later years however this was more likely to have been done by craftsmen in a boatyard, during a time of overhaul and repair. But there are still many honourable exceptions, both amateur and professional. Even men working in the boatyards are often descended from canal families, either boaters or boatbuilders, and are steeped in the folklore of the waterways. They would at first learn their skills through trial and error or by watching more experienced workers, but in later years there have been genuine apprenticeship schemes.

Since the Second World War there have even been a few men and women with art school training to help to keep the tradition of canal decoration alive, though they have been mainly concerned with renovation of pleasure craft and the sale of cans and other utensils as souvenirs. Some misguided critics have deplored this trend, mistaking facility and knowledge for mere slickness. They hanker after the 'good old days' when real canal paintings were produced, admiring mistakes and blemishes as much as self-confidence and boldness of attack. Such critics forget that even the time-honoured crafts are bound to undergo some form of change, imperceptible as this may seem to the novice. An influx of new blood and ideas may help rather than hinder, provided the student from outside is willing to understand and absorb the background of his medium, using commonsense to sift what is sincere and genuine from what is false and trivial. This is not to stand the craft on its head, to dispense with established modes of work; neither is it a slavish copying of earlier examples, as if one dreaded to lose the feeling of naïvety.

There are many obvious difficulties in store, for both highly trained and untrained but sincere craftsmen, in boat decoration and other canal arts. While the untutored or badly trained worker is hampered by limitations of knowledge and ability, the more sophisticated are slowed down, if not inhibited, by limitations of a crude, almost clumsy medium. A work, perhaps close to the accepted ideal, may please by its dash and boldness of concept while affronting aesthetic taste with innocent perspective and architectural solecism. This may be balanced, in another work, by a self-conscious effort in which lines vanish at the correct angles and details relate to the whole but seem academic and niggling. In seeking a middle course it may be necessary to establish the difference between errors and conventions, making use of whatever short cuts conform with an overall sense of design without impeding essential liveliness and spontaneity.

Once committed to a scheme of decoration the average boater begrudges neither time nor money to see that the work is carried out according to the highest standards. It is important to remember however that, while most boat families take a pride in their craft and the innocent pleasures of one-upmanship, there was formerly a practical side to boat decoration. From the days when checking boats, granting licences and inspecting living quarters came into force it was the smartly painted, neatly kept boat that stood a better chance of acceptance.

Boats are painted both externally and internally, in common with most items of furnishings, utensils and fittings. Dealing with external features first: it will be noted that bright colours are usually limited to areas above the gunwale. The hull is a background of solid black, suitable for showing off gay colours or decorations on the upper works by contrast. The general pattern of decoration is fairly standard throughout the country but with minor variations of mainly local or commercial significance.

The upper parts of the prow or stem post are frequently painted scarlet. Inward-curving lines running back from the bows towards the stern continue as far as the cratch. These usually form an enclosed band along the gunwale in which swags of roses might appear, the area terminated by diamond, crescent or scalloped shapes. The band is usually painted in light colours with darker outlining.

One of the outstanding features of the forepart is the triangular front board or cratch. This is usually painted with either geometrical figures, known as 'shapes', the familiar roses or a combination of both. A typical scheme of decoration in this respect would be for a double vertical band of vertical shapes to occupy the centre of the cratch, supported on each side by equally spaced triangles, each containing an arrangement of six or more roses. An outer edge of the bands and triangles would be outlined in a contrasting colour, frequently a straw yellow or dark green with a red or blue background. As previously mentioned, the cratch of a Barlow boat was often one of its most colourful features of decoration. During later years, from the mid-1930s, a few boats used the cratch to advertise branded products of the firms for which they worked, foremost among these being Ovaltine and Cadbury's chocolate.

The interior of the cargo space is usually painted an overall coat of red oxide, although this is soon stained and discoloured by cargo and rough usage. Uprights are frequently green or red, with red predominating. On some early boats stands and masts were black and white. Upper parts of verticals usually have bands of diamonds or lozenges in contrasting colours. Part of the top planks, especially the downward bend resting on the cabin block, is painted with lozenges and triangles of red, green, yellow and white. The spare top plank is also painted with diamonds. Running blocks for the towing ropes usually have chamfered or mock-chamfered edges and are painted in light colours outlined in darker or contrasting pigments.

Cabin roofs are frequently treated with an effect of wood graining, either light or dark oak but usually the former. Slides and deck lids are decorated with a playing card motif, such as the ace of clubs or hearts, with the borders of each slide surrounded by arcs of colour or lined out in green, blue or red. The sides of the main or stern cabin, sloping inwards towards the centre, are divided into two or three neat panels. One of the larger panels contains the owner's name, business address and similar details. A smaller panel at either cargo or cockpit end might frame a view of a traditional castle set in a background of romantic scenery. On most boats the pictorial motif is usually at the stern end. A further small panel contains the registration number. Most side panels are surrounded by an area of wood graining.

The stern bulkhead of the living cabin is partly occupied by double doors, usually left open and hinged back in the daytime but closed at night. While the interiors of the doors are panelled, the exterior is flush with the rest of the bulkhead, the whole being painted in two main colours divided by a narrow band of lighter colour in the form of an arabesque. The main colours are frequently red or blue and green, lined out with yellow or white, the sinuous contour (originally sketched out with a few chalk marks) having an almost oriental character.

A tapering band of light colour, usually white, complementary to a similar band at the bows, follows the curve of the gunwale from cabin space to steerage. This provides a place for the name of the boat, sometimes with a motif of rope and anchor (a fouled anchor) near the stern post, although in recent years this was frequently omitted. Beyond the name space, looking forward, the coloured band changes to a pattern of lozenges running for three-quarters the length of the cabin side. It is terminated with a crescent moon or by a sun placed next to a quarter or crescent moon. Odd corners are filled with patterns of roses, daisies or just shapes. Scrolls, crescents, fleur-de-lys and miniature playing card designs are sometimes painted in the centres of the lozenges. Beneath the lower line of the name band near the stern a triangular panel, painted red or blue, encloses a swag of roses or mixed roses and daisies.

(*Left*) Butty deck lid

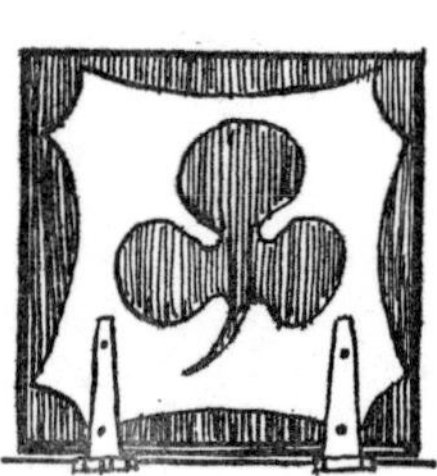

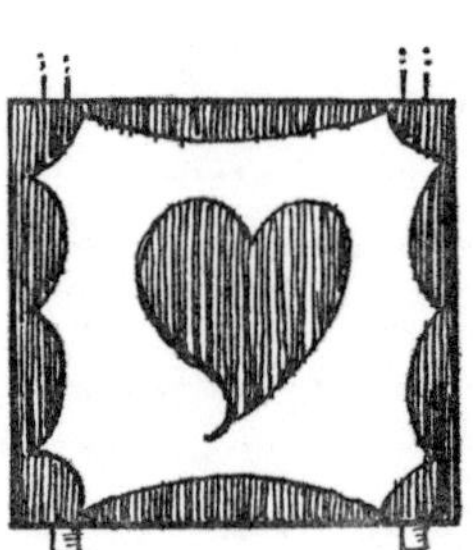

(*Right*) Cabin slide

One of the most characteristic and aesthetically pleasing features of the butty is the tall rudder post known as the ram's head, formerly decorated with the flowing tail of a grey horse. This is painted in several contrasting colours, the woodwork being in many cases chamfered at the edges. It is also noted for its decorative ropework, the upper bands of which are interwoven to resemble an eastern turban or 'Turk's head'. The top of the ram's head is usually painted red or green, but sometimes red, white and blue. Areas of colour curve down on each side to a part where iron bands reinforce the tiller socket. Other sections of the same structure are covered with small shapes or panels as far down as the rudder blade. Below the line of an almost horizontal brace the boarding of the rudder is painted jet black or treated with tar dressings. A small circular motif might also appear on each side of the ram's head, occasionally topped and tailed by a swag of roses or a flourish of brush strokes.

The bow-shaped tiller is carved with eight separate sides or facets which vary in width, four being wide and four narrow. These taper to a convenient hand grip, different surfaces sometimes lined out in contrasting colours. The extremity of the tiller, at the cabin end, is smooth and rounded, while at the stern end it is squared off to fit a socket of the ram's head.

Designs and colours on the power boat are intended to match those of the butty, but are frequently less elaborate than those of the traditional craft. The main exception is in the painting of the tiller handle, which in the case of the power boat is a metal rod striped to resemble a barber's pole. The effect of regular diagonal stripes is achieved by winding a piece of thread dipped in paint round the entire length of the tiller. This establishes the first line, which is easy enough to follow with a fine brush for subsequent lines. Dark lines are usually contrasted with lighter bands of colour. The small engine room hatch or pigeon box normally has a pattern of roses at each end and diamonds along both sides.

Pigeon box (*top*) and lift-off type box

When side doors leading into the engine hole are made of wood they are panelled and decorated in the traditional style, although left plain if made of iron or steel. Side panels abaft the engine hole, on the outer walls of the cabin, display the name and address of the carrying firm or owner, also the name of the boat, roses being used as convenient space fillers. Panels or bands on the counter stern are painted in the house colours favoured by a particular firm, although the upper band is usually red.

The sides of a power boat cabin frequently have one or more brass-rimmed portholes. A single port sometimes appears on the tumblehome of a butty cabin, with a bullseye or convex glass set in the middle of the stern cabin roof.

Stern bulkhead of butty

Roses and castles

It is claimed that great mystery surrounds the traditional roses and castles, so long a feature of narrow boat decoration. As many theories have been advanced relating to their origins as those concerning the first canal families.

Many experts assert that castle motifs are essentially oriental or at least Carpathian, hinting at much-travelled gipsy origins of early boaters and canal workers. Others detect the likeness of Windsor or even Tamworth castles, either from excessive loyalty or because, in the case of Tamworth, this was a landmark near the centre of the waterway system. Strangely enough boaters on the navigations of the Potteries and West Midlands frequently substituted farm houses or country cottages for dream castles.

One theory traces the origin of castle towers to the high kilns (bottle kilns) seen in many industrial areas. The bottle kilns were used in both the glass industry of the Black Country (between Stourbridge and Brierley Hill) and the earthenware manufacture of the Potteries. Tall, narrow minaret-like towers could be developed from the chimney stacks of factory and mill. Flags or pennants floating from battlements might be interpretations of plumes of smoke or steam from engine houses. The mountainous settings of the castles could be suggested by the spoil tips and waste mounds of mine and quarry.

Whatever their origins in fact or fancy, most of the castles appear make-believe structures, nearer Balmoral and the Victorian or romantic ideal than medieval reality. It is unlikely that any of their fanciful towers could withstand more than a token siege, having nothing in common with the grim world of battering rams, scaling ladders and boiling pitch. It is possible they represented more than patriotic ideals or past memories, proving aspirations towards a more comfortable place in the world with room to expand and breath in literal terms. The bane of the boater's life was the cramped and restricted atmosphere of the stern cabin. Cosy and convenient it may have seemed on a winter night, but there was scarcely room to sneeze without dislodging some cherished ornament or fitting. What more could the frustrated boater desire that to contemplate the largest of all human dwellings, the castle? To an individual giving free rein to his fancies only a castle proved grand enough, especially as an alternative to an undersized floating home. The average boater might well have reflected that the total area of cabin space was scarcely larger than a massive sideboard or buffet in mock baronial halls of the period. It was perhaps significant that painted castles should often have more than their share of windows and doorways, everything that might be lacking in a stern cabin. Some of the castles had strange onion-shaped domes, similar to those of Russian churches, which seem more theatrical than authentic.

Most castles were painted in a park-like setting, with feathery trees, winding paths and broad expanses of water, yet bordering wild or mountainous country. While part of the foreground might be occupied by a casual stream, often changing to the castle moat, this in turn flowed into a lake or estuary with elegant yachts tacking towards the sunset. Tumbled hills and even a mountain range of almost volcanic grandeur filled odd spaces of the background, taller peaks being sometimes wreathed in clouds or snow drifts. These improbable uplands added to a feeling of seclusion and romance while helping to bind the composition together, avoiding difficulties of perspective encountered in a flat terrain. While some of the canals on the Pennines passed through or near rugged country most of the inland network was surrounded by flat meadows and low horizons, so that the excitement of crag and mountain, forest and glen was as much wishful thinking in pictorial terms as the design of dream castles. It was frequently impossible to define where trees merged into hills or water touched land. Yet mistiness and diffusion were not always due to lack of technical skill and may serve to hint at dreamlike, unworldly settings far removed from a life spent crouching over hard-edged furniture or staring at enclosed meadows of chessboard regularity.

The castles and their romantic backgrounds were certainly a change from the small fields and game coverts of Warwickshire, Northamptonshire or other homely counties. Perhaps the nearest point of reality to this dreamworld was the solitary mass of Beeston Crag with its ruined keep, which dominates the Cheshire Plain and may be viewed from the upper reaches of the Shropshire Union Canal. Yet to the puritan cloud castles suggested pomp and vanity, so that nonconformist boaters of the Potteries often turned their ambitions towards country cottages and small holdings. Even here an unquestioned aspiration for more living space may be seen.

Despite both commonsense and fanciful explanations the painting of castles will always remain something of a mystery. Painting roses however was a predictable mode of expression from the earliest days. The forms of plants and flowers have long been important, even basic, ingredients of most creative pattern making, pre-dating acanthus leaf motifs of Greece and Rome or the hibiscus and lotus flowers of Egyptian temples. Bud, blossom and leaf are ideal space fillers, being adapted to many interpretations from naturalistic to semi-abstract. It is far from coincidence that so many Victorian amateurs were flower painters or began their training for the visual arts with these particular subjects. Apart from their charming simplicity and graceful proportions, flower and plant forms touch so nearly the abstract principles of symmetry, rhythm and harmony without even hinting at vexed questions of perspective, spatial depth and emotional content.

Roses were first chosen as a pictorial subject by canal folk because they could be adapted to so many different shapes, schemes and surfaces without too much sacrifice of naturalism. They symbolised a degree of luxury and gracious living at which the painting of castles also hinted. There is also the

Rose.

Each petal a brushstroke.

Leaf

Veins thicken towards outer edges.

Sun flower with leaves. Brush strokes round edges serve as space fillers.

probability that roses of a sort were grown round the porches or in the gardens of lockside cottages, while dog roses rambled freely in hedges bordering towing paths. The only other flower widely used as a pictorial motif is the humble daisy, familiar enough along canal banks and near backwaters. The painter of canal boats is thus influenced not only by dreams and fancies but also by things observed in everyday life. Both types of flower are sometimes mingled in wreath or swag, although tending to look slightly incongruous when daisies are too large or appear to outnumber roses. Roses and daisies, especially roses, are universal on canals, decorating not only side panels of cabins but also water cans, dippers, stools and a variety of other fittings.

While few painters stray from roses and daisies, lilies of the valley and crude attempts at arum lily and iris are not entirely unknown. Blue trumpet-shaped flowers sometimes appear on the interior walls of boat cabins where it may be difficult to distinguish between an overgrown daisy and a small sunflower.

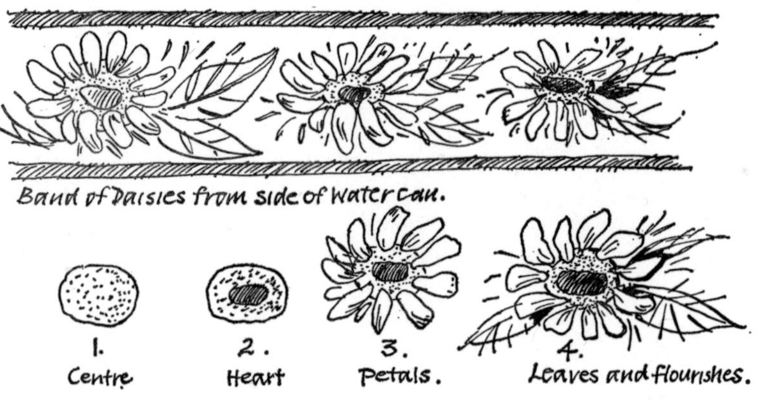

Stages in painting a daisy

Good luck symbols and similar motifs

Boaters and canal folk in general, being close to nature in their daily lives, are often obsessed by the need for good luck, usually meaning fair weather, and many pictorial motifs, apart from roses and castles, may be classed as good luck symbols or tokens. These include playing card designs such as the ace of clubs, heart shapes, nautical anchors and the lucky clover leaf. The majority of these are seldom painted on side panels or hull, although anchors rightly belong to the name band near the stern post. They are mainly used to decorate such fittings as deck lids or slides. Most of them, especially anchors, began to disappear or decline in popularity shortly after the Second World War. Another symbol of good luck, the tail of a grey horse fixed to the ram's head of the butty, also disappeared during the same period although it was to be expected that with the decline of horses there would also be a shortage of tails. The passing of anchors may be deeply regretted as a pair of these, one on each side of the stern gunwales, treated with almost heraldic precision, added a touch of distinction to almost any craft.

The 'Staffordshire knot' was occasionally seen in the Black Country area, mainly on day boats, but was far from universal. It mainly appeared as a corner filler on side panels.

Geometrical figures and patterns

A third category of boat painting relates to the use of geometrical figures and patterns, known as 'shapes'. These mainly appear on masts, stands, blocks and cratches. The commencement of top planks or gangplanks at the stern end, also blocks on which they rest, are often decorated in this abstract or geometrical style. This comprises either regular borders and patterns of lining out, or round, square and diamond shapes used as space fillers, contrasting with freely painted roses and castles (free in both style and content). A simple arrangement of dice and lozenge is perhaps the most popular motif in this style and may be inserted in awkward spaces, between gangplanks and the heads of stands, which might inhibit a more painterly technique. A pattern of lozenges is frequently known in this connection as 'plaiding' or 'Scotch plaid'. Moon, sun and stars, especially the crescent moon, are treated as simple shapes or geometrical figures. The latter are usually confined to gunwales and name bands at stern and prow.

One of the most delightful yet simple motifs is a small disc pattern, appearing on both name band and ram's head. This is designed with arcs and curves, filled in with primary colours, to resemble the petals of a daisy. For want of a better description it may be termed a 'compass wheel'. There are six petal shapes in all, the circumference of the enclosing disc or circle being outlined with a band of dark paint, as are individual petals. Spaces for and between the petals could account for up to four colours, including white.

Arabesques painted on the outer or stern bulkhead of the living cabin are unique and exotic, representing a rare feat of geometrical design. A similar but less exacting pattern is sometimes painted on the near horizontal boards of the after deck, between hatches and ram's head. This latter however is frequently hidden by a protective canvas cover, also used to protect the name band.

Rococo embellishments and flourishes similar to painted designs and gilded plasterwork ornaments of the eighteenth century, before the chilling influence of the Adam style, are sometimes used as fillers in conjunction with name bands and spaces at the stern ends of canal craft. Lozenges and full and crescent moons are used far more frequently however for the same purpose. It may be noted that skilfully painted lettering fulfils an important role in the general design scheme, a matter considered in a later chapter.

A matter of comparisons

It may be claimed that painters of narrow boats are far more limited in their technical approach than other popular artists such as painters of fairground and circus equipment. The showman painter, in designing fascia or rounding boards for sideshows and roundabouts, appears in a superficial sense to display a greater imagination than his counterpart of the inland waterways. Chariot races, boxing matches and combats between wild beasts are far removed from the peaceful world of cabbage roses and dream castles. Fairground painters have long been renowned for their ability to tackle almost any subject from the charge of the Light Brigade to launching a battleship, taking portraits of film stars, famous generals and popular statesmen in their stride. Their apparent knowledge of historical costume, architecture and animal anatomy would have confounded many exhibitors at the Victorian Royal Academy. Yet allowing credit where it may be due, the work of the showman painter is much nearer the aims of the commercial artist and illustrator of the old school than those of the true artist. Even the finest examples of the fairground are inspired by needs of crude publicity, so that superficial cleverness rather than sincerity of design and depth of feeling may set a limit to their creative endeavours. A work of art at any level cannot be measured in terms of sheer bulk and complexity. For this reason the fairground painting over the entrance to a sideshow is less a genuine folk work than paintings on a canal boat. Both showmen and boaters lead a roving life but showmen tend to mix far more with crowds than canal dwellers. The showman is also influenced to a greater extent by a wide range of pictorial matter, including posters, magazine illustrations and newspapers, with which the canal dweller is rarely in contact.

Many of the spectacular scenes of the fairground are versions of similar works reproduced in magazines and lurid newspaper supplements by a wide range of popular illustrators. Portraits of film stars and other celebrities have been lifted straight from cigarette cards and picture postcards. The painter of canal boats, perhaps too naïve to copy in detail, is not merely held captive by the traditions of his craft, but is far more limited to an original point of view. This may seem a contradiction in terms when remembering the limits of subject matter involved. Yet no two castles are alike, and however crude the technique employed, most side panel and similar decorations are usually painted with an assurance lacking in other popular arts. The fairground painter also makes frequent use of templates and other mechanical aids for decorative work, ploys that self-respecting canal painters might view with contempt.

Perhaps the nearest the boater came to betraying an aesthetic trust was during the world wars when flags of the allied nations sometimes appeared in place of arabesque and lozenge. The main discernible influence to which boat painters succumbed may well have been toy theatre scenery and backdrops. Romantic castles and mountain scenery were the stock in trade of most theatrical painters, and popular enough on both 'penny plain or twopence coloured' sheets or canvas flats during this time to influence even remote canal dwellers. The travelling theatre, 'gaff' or 'blood tub' was a popular institution of the Victorian era, especially in the Midlands, and may have been visited by boaters when pitched on wasteland near the canalside.* Yet if such influences are genuine they were exceptions to prove the rule and less hampering to genuine self-expression than the cover of a 'penny dreadful'.

To appreciate the art of the canal painter it is essential to see not merely individual paintings or details but the decoration of the craft as a whole. The narrow boat may be termed a satisfying object in its own right with painted ornaments evolved to enhance its fitness for purpose. Roses and castles however are sometimes introduced to the structural surfaces of other vessels including pleasure yachts and cabin cruisers; they have even been known to penetrate bars of canalside inns and ornament doors or side panels of trailer caravans and motor vehicles. Yet seen out of context, even on a boat of the wrong shape, such designs lose meaning and impact. Buying or even commissioning works of this type, divorced from their original setting, makes a fascinating hobby but has little to do with the traditions of genuine folk art.

The painting of large scale side panels on the exteriors of canal craft underwent a decline during the period between

* The author has vivid memories of such a travelling show pitched near the Coventry Canal during the mid-1930s. A rare survival.

the world wars. The chief enthusiasts for this mode of display were the 'number ones' or owner-boaters, of whom there were still a fair number up to and during the First World War. These men would either paint their own boats from end to end or spend large sums on having the job done professionally in a canalside boatyard. Keeping the family boat in good order and painted in the correct style was part of the boater's creed, concerning which 'number ones' proved natural leaders of style and taste. Unfortunately during the depression years of the late twenties and early thirties very few of the owner-boaters could afford to remain in business and sold their craft to large haulage firms, the latter able to stay afloat through amalgamations and strict economy. Most 'number ones' lacked capital or business sense to weather hard times and where they stayed on the canals it was either to handle the boats of other men or to work in repair yards.

For reasons of both taste and economy carrying companies tended to reduce the painting of narrow boats to a simple house livery. There was no intention in most cases of budgeting for such foibles as roses and castles, which were relegated to interior designs and the inner panels of doors leading into the stern cabin. These were often on a smaller scale than exterior panels and could be painted by the boaters themselves in odd if infrequent moments of leisure. For those remaining afloat, either as hired crews or owner-boaters, the pressure was soon greatly increased with a return to grinding competition. Rules and regulations may well have been flaunted for the sake of trade, although boaters were rarely known for regular hours or careful living at any time. Even when working company boats almost deprived of external decorations, and unable to spend much time painting their own fittings, they frequently bought hand-painted items on a crude hire purchase system from canalside shops, paying a few shillings or pence when passing through the area. In this way boaters were at least enabled to sport the components of a colourful interior or cabin roof with certain items such as dipper and water can being displayed on the roof as a long-established tradition.

The official stinginess of the carrying companies in this department was at first continued by British Waterways after nationalisation. For a number of years all commercial craft owned by the waterways, mainly absorbed from the larger haulage firms, were forced to appear in a livery of custard yellow and electric blue, colours rarely popular with the majority of boaters. Individual tastes were confined to water cans and interiors, although even on cabin doors official transfers were encouraged rather than hand paintings. It may be noted that the transfers in question, issued in several sizes, were designed by Frank Jones, a boat painter of Leighton Buzzard. These restrictions were relaxed even before the Waterways Board decided to dispose of their fleet, and the boaters who remained on the canals lost no time in reinstating traditional modes.

Part two: The Art

During their heyday the smartest narrow boats were painted every two years. This was usually done when the boat was docked for overhaul or when it might be needed as the honeymoon home of newly wed canal folk. Under ideal circumstances a boat might dock after 12 months for a general check up and 'black round' with tar dressings. Two years later there would be a more extensive treatment, often with external and internal painting of all parts. Although four years between total repaints was considered the maximum for self-respect, during years of decline docking periods were spaced further apart, sometimes reaching an interval of five years and upwards. This routine did not prevent individual boaters from repainting or touching up either structural or interior fittings according to whim.

While some canal painters are obviously better at producing landscapes or swags of roses for side panels, others may specialise in decorating such items as dippers, water cans and nose bowls. The average dock painter however is usually more versatile, in technical scope if not in subject matter and treatment, while some boaters find it easier to express themselves in a limited sphere and feign unwillingness to venture beyond utensils or small scale work.

It may be noted that painted water cans were eventually

Spouted water can and dippers

sold in canalside shops and boat chandlers, these being produced by a talented storekeeper with an eye to the customer. Water cans produced at Long Buckby on the Grand Union Canal were renowned for sturdy qualities of design and cheerful colouring, much sought after by the average boater. Even today experts are able to distinguish between different styles of work and may recognise a vintage Long Buckby or Braunston can at a glance. This relates more to individual touch than to variations of design, each craftsman producing what amounts to a personal handwriting in paint.

As with many folk arts individual craftsmen tend to be modest and anonymous. A few significant names emerge however, including Nurser of Braunston, Tooley of Banbury and Frank Jones of Leighton Buzzard (designer of the British Waterways transfer). Yet it should not be thought that decoration of canal craft is a thing of the past. While a few veterans such as Ron Hough of Braunston Dock preserve an unbroken tradition there are also numbers of younger folk worthy to prove their successors, and there are increasing demands from amateur boaters.

Perhaps the main difference between the workmanship of past and present lies, with notable exceptions, in the bolder yet more casual approach of former days. One disadvantage of a craft now partly supported by amateurs is that canal painters tend to become self-conscious, frequently lacking the gusto and joy in self-expression of their predecessors. Increased technical skill may to a certain extent replace lost innocence and spontaneity, but while this is by no means the disadvantage it at first seems new trends reveal themselves alongside both conservative traditions and changing methods. At one time a panel was expected to withstand weather and rough usage but seldom to survive decades or generations. We are fortunate that examples of canal paintings have been preserved for our inspiration from the earlier days, although when they were painted the work was seldom considered serious enough to be permanent. Modern versions of the same themes are now produced to last, greater care and restraint being taken in their execution and with quality materials used at all stages of the work. It is an ever-increasing conflict to reconcile freshness and freedom with an hitherto unfelt need for permanence and stability. On the debit side canal painting, in common with many other arts, has lost something of its masculine vigour through over refinement.

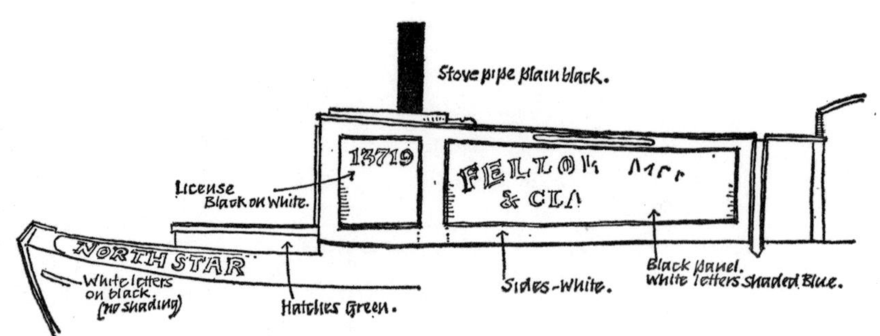

Original colour scheme of Fellows,
Morton and Clayton boats

Allocation of colours on exteriors of narrow boats

Hull	Black with white or straw coloured lining out. Details and lining out at prow and stern also in scarlet and blue. Flowers on hull at prow and stern: red and yellow (green leaves).
Cratch	Scarlet or green. Lined out with white or straw colour. Also front board plain red and unlined. Bands of diamonds in red (usually dark red), green, white, blue, yellow.
Running Blocks	Usually blue and white or red and white. Sometimes black and white.
Mast and Stands	Green, red, white, black. Bands of diamonds in yellow, white and red.
Deck Lid	Ace of Clubs, etc, red, black on white with dark green borders.
Snakes	Decorative iron-work at prow painted black. Nailed to blue background. Enclosed within bands of white and red.
Rudder Post	Red, blue, white, cream or straw colour. Green sometimes added. Rudder blade usually black.
Tiller	Yellowish cream (Naples yellow) or straw colour, dark red and blue.
Lettering at the Stern End	Red, orange. Shaded light yellow, brown and black. Background in dark blue and/or red with white lining out.

The above may be considered average or preferred colours, popular with boaters until the introduction of a standard blue and yellow livery after nationalisation. There were, however, many variations, especially of detail, too numerous to record.

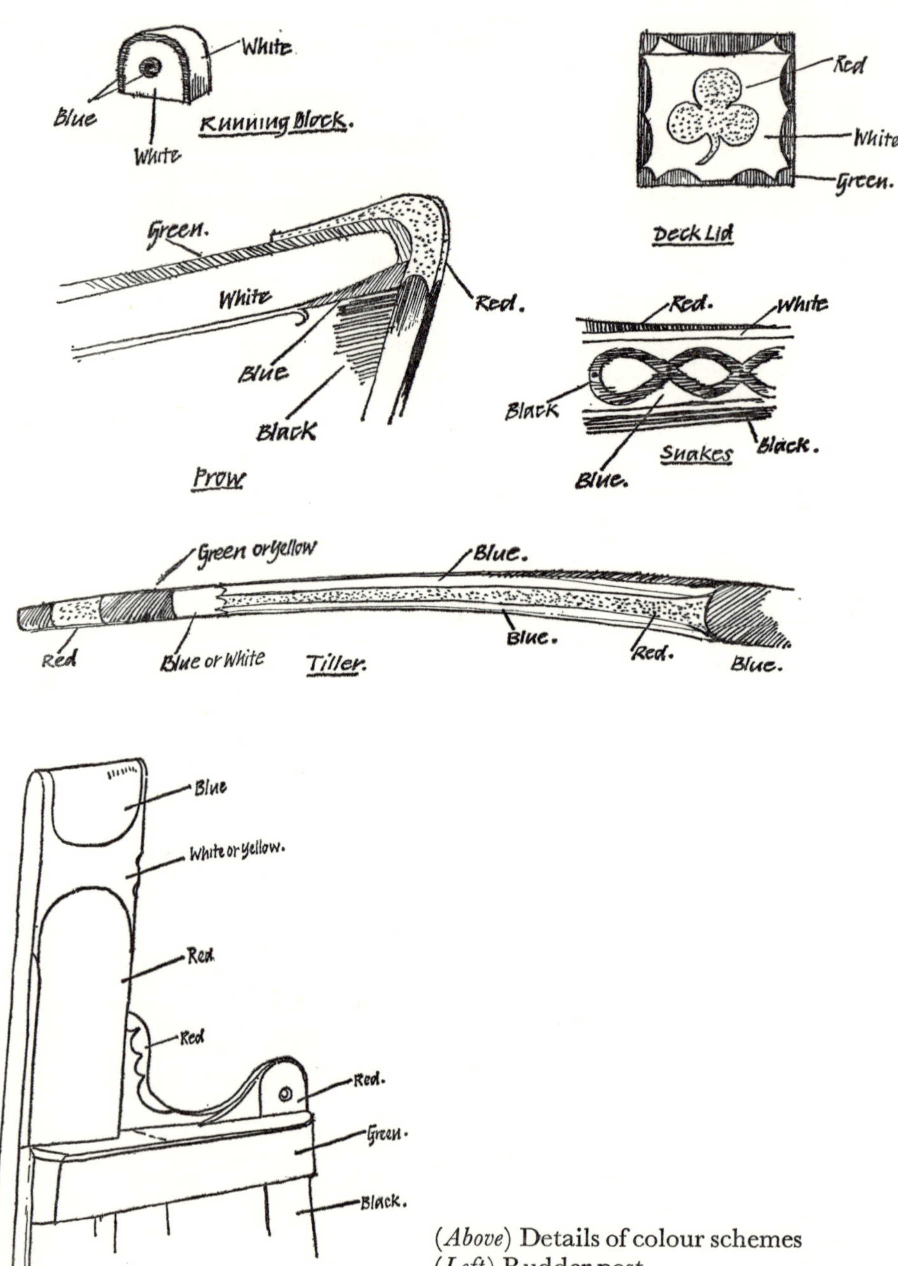

(*Above*) Details of colour schemes
(*Left*) Rudder post

Painting the boat

In former days it was probable that one man, frequently the owner-boater, would paint or at least decorate the entire craft and its fittings. In the boatyards a single craftsman might be assisted by an apprentice. Later practice frequently involved several members of a team or family group working on different parts of the same boat. One might paint floral decorations, another lettering, a third landscapes and castles. Such an order of work is by no means uncommon among contemporary painters.

Working at a level easy rate, skilled craftsmen may finish the decoration of a narrow boat in a day. This is all the more remarkable when as many as 300 roses alone adorn a single craft. To paint an entire boat from stem to stern, allowing for drying out of undercoats, takes at least three or four days. Drying time for complete works vary according to weather and season but may take up to eight days. Painting a motor boat is a slightly longer task than painting a butty. During post-war years, when many boatyards closed under economic pressure, smaller carrying companies were known to contract out to ordinary house painters, decorations in such cases being either limited or non-existent.

By a strange paradox traditional designs and standards are more closely followed in boatyards than by individual boaters. The dock painter, frequently serving a long apprenticeship, is even more conservative than the boat dweller. Despite his respect for tradition the more adventurous boater sometimes experiments with motifs other than roses and castles, including churches, wooded landscapes and groups of buildings meant to represent the distant view of a canal town. Birds fluttering round the branch of a tree appear on interior panels while the heads of dogs or horses are sometimes displayed on utensils. Yet roses and castles, with the exception of farmhouses and cottages in the north and west Midlands, are the accepted norm on all waterways. However much artistry might be employed in painting the head of a favourite bull terrier, it is after all a matter of personal taste with which many may be unable to agree. The dock painter cannot risk offending his customers by departing from time-honoured rules, whatever his own ideas happen to be.

No particular type of paint is used, much depending on individual tastes and the availability of materials. Flat paints are preferred, of a quality used for outdoor structures, with emphasis on durability. They may be supplied either in tins or as finely ground powder, to be mixed in linseed oil, thinned out with oils or spirits or sometimes a mixture of both. Hand mixing and grinding of colours was frequently practised by many of the older generation of dock painters, for both preference and economy, but this tradition declined during the past 30 years. Some modern painters however prefer to mix if not to grind their own colours, in order to obtain an effect of greater depth and brilliance. Paint supplied in tins, usually for covering purposes, contains more than its share of white, but this tends to dull normal pigments. Ordinary marine paints and varnishes are the solution for external fittings, although superior quality enamel paint is now frequently used for interior work, water cans and small utensils. Modern painters sometimes prefer oil-ground pigments of artists' quality for internal landscapes, while using signwriters' colours for lettering and external details. Some painters, usually boaters, are known to break all the rules by mixing gloss with non-gloss paints of different qualities, results appearing effective for at least a limited period. To work quickly, almost informally, is certainly in the waterways tradition, touching up or repainting being a casual affair fitted in as time allows.

Brushes vary in size, softness or hardness of bristle and in length of handle according to the amount of detail required. Many boat painters, especially professionals, equip themselves with a fair number of different types and sizes, some preferring to use a brush for each colour. As the work becomes smaller and finer brushes need to be more pointed and flexible, usually camel or ox hair rather than hog bristle. Modern painters of cans and utensils frequently use the more delicate brushes of watercolour painters (numbered '1', '2', '5' and '6'), often of pure sable hair. Numbers, an indication of size and fineness, are usually marked on the handles. The finest quality sable brush is an expensive item of equipment and seldom bought by boaters wishing to touch up a water can or panel. For such work they may be content with anything supplied by the corner shop, ranging from a child's paint brush in camel or squirrel hair to a flat-bristled nondescript type normally used for slapping paint on a garden gate.

Other items of equipment are simple and limited. They include graining combs, a block of pumice stone, a few empty cans for mixing and dipping, a scraping knife, a small lump of putty, odd lengths of wood or old brush handles for stirring, a length of chalked string, thinners in bottle or can, a piece of flat wood for trying out (useful but not essential) and quantities of rags for cleaning. Many of these things may be salvaged from scrap. The average boater may even limit his gear to brushes, paint and a couple of old cans.

Application of paint on new woodwork includes the usual process of 'knotting', 'stopping' and laying at least three coats of oil-based colours. Knotting means covering wood knots with shellac mixture dissolved in spirits, to prevent gum resin exuding from knots and cracks and discolouring finished paintwork. Stopping is the preventive filling of large cracks, deep nail holes and crevices made by loosely fitting joints; it is mainly done with putty and paint. Knotting is completed before the first application of undercoat while stopping is tackled after priming. To cover old work depends very much on the state of the under surface. It is often sufficient merely to wash down with warm water, wipe dry and pumice away rougher areas.

Graining, mainly for cabin interiors, cabin roofs, the inner surfaces of double doors and borders round side panels, is usually the imitation of natural oak in light tones. Dark oak is far less popular than lighter shades and seldom used. Having applied the undercoat a ground colour of the correct tint is added and left to dry. In the meantime a preparation which includes boiled linseed oil, turpentine and a small quantity of brown paint is laid over an appropriate work area. A clean flat brush of hog bristle is then dipped in the mixture and dragged through newly laid colour. Whorls and mottled areas are picked out with softer brushes and left to dry. Combs of different sizes may be used for the same purpose, the finished effect in this case known as 'combing'. Steel, wooden and even cardboard combs are used, some preferring the familiar toilet comb with its sharp teeth protected by thin cloth. For additional realism the same surface may be double-grained. Final protection is given by one or two coats of copal varnish.

Most straight work is either executed in lean tones (thinned out with spirits over a neutral undercoat) or by direct painting on to a primed wooden surface. Finished painting may be varnished after a suitable drying out period. Some boat panels and fittings are re-varnished dozens of times, eventually turning a dull brown since the varnish used is not always of the best quality and is sometimes insufficiently protected from dust during its drying period. Caught at what might be called the right age some designs appear to improve with mellowing and maturity, qualities once admired in the old masters of easel painting.

There is rarely any set order of work for painting castles and landscapes. Preliminary sketches and studies common to a majority of artists are totally lacking. Except for wanging a chalked string, known as a 'snap line', for straight lines, borders and lettering patterns, there are no further guides or attempts at drawing distinct from brushwork. Very few descend to the use of hand rests such as the mahlstick (a long shaft the end of which is fitted with a cloth-covered knob; used by easel painters to steady hand and wrist). In this respect the traditional canal boat painter is as self-reliant as an impressionist, scorning the props and preparations once forming a vital part of studio and art school training. Full use however is frequently made, for decorative effect, of grain marks and cracks in a surface.

The nearest approach to formality in landscape painting lies in the fact that most artists prefer to start with the sky, working from top to bottom rather than the other way round. Sky in the background and water in the foreground are frequently painted together using the same colours, much of the sky seeming reflected in moat, river or lake. The basic colour for skyscapes is often dark blue, near to Prussian blue, at the top and edges, modified by the addition of white, to merge from dark to light and back to darker tones at the foot of the panel. Pinks and yellows for sunsets are blended into the sky during the early stages. While some painters add clouds and other details when the underpainting is touch dry, others prefer to overpaint before the first brush strokes have dried out, in order to obtain a melting or blending effect. The latter is known as 'bleeding' the colours, one pigment tending to pick up another rather than remaining separate. Raw colours are mixed directly on the painting surface rather than on a palette.

Many paint sky, water, mountains (a green undercoat for fields in the foreground, with trees in the middle distance, and then superficial details) in that order. Others dash in the sky then work outwards from the centre of vision near the middle of the picture, painting castles and bridges before dealing with grass. No hard and fast rules can be made but the general trend is to paint from top to bottom and from centre to outer edges. Main buildings such as castles tend to be slightly to left or right of centre in the middle distance, with bridges nearer the foreground, appearing more to the opposite side. Mountains serve as a backdrop while trees, bushes, rocks and winding paths are used either as 'lead ins' or space fillers.

Any type of brush may be used to obtain the right effect. Old and nearly worn out signwriters' brushes, no longer suitable for lettering, are often favoured. Failing everything else it is by no means uncommon for a canal painter to smear or dab with thumb and forefinger. Yet while fingers are excellent painting tools the brush is preferred whenever possible for its lively pattern of bristle marks.

For painting broad masses a juicy well-diluted paint is preferred, few canal painters feeling at home with stiff or dry pigments. For painting details of landscapes and castles a sepia tint is often detected in both shading and outlines. This serves the two-fold purpose of emphasising certain parts of the picture while adding strength and clarity to the foreground. Outlining is used to separate planes and masses where the painter is hampered by weak draughtsmanship and unable to express three dimensions through ignorance of perspective.

From the design aspect it is difficult to find major faults. Although canal painters seldom involve themselves in complex problems of design and composition they at least show commendable taste in avoiding such matters by appearing to know their limitations. Fortunately the average canal painter appears to have an instinctive feeling for layout and arrangement; here he is perhaps helped rather than impeded by life and work in a confined space. The life of the inland waterways is essentially enclosed, both in stern cabin and boatyard, the narrowness of typical English canals adding greatly to their visual appeal. This compromise with space is bound to influence those in daily contact with such scenes.

One aspect of sound practice from most viewpoints lies in the boat painter's ability to achieve maximum effect with each brush stroke. This implies a mastery and control, informing brushwork with a liveliness and interest for its own sake. The touch of the average canal painter is light, uninhibited and refreshing, in fine contrast to the laboured efforts of many amateurs or imitators. At least part of the secret may lie in the fact that boat painting is an end or pleasure in itself.

When roses are painted on panels, usually as space fillers, they are applied to a dry matt surface. Brush marks are even more evident in flower paintings than in landscapes.

It is frequently claimed that styles of painting in the north tend to be stronger, brighter but less finished than those in the south.

Oil navigation lamp

F.M.C. steamer passing through a lock *c.* 1898. The women are wearing traditional costume but fashionable hats rather than bonnets

A steamer and her crew *c.* 1900

Stern of a butty boat

Castle on door panel of stern cabin

Rare painting on canvas cover used to decorate interior of stern cabin

Modern version of the castle

Name panel with shaded lettering on stern cabin of motorboat

Decoration on gunwale of narrow boat

Later stage of painting a decorative panel with detailed added

Rudder post showing details of rope work and painting. Note the compass wheel motif

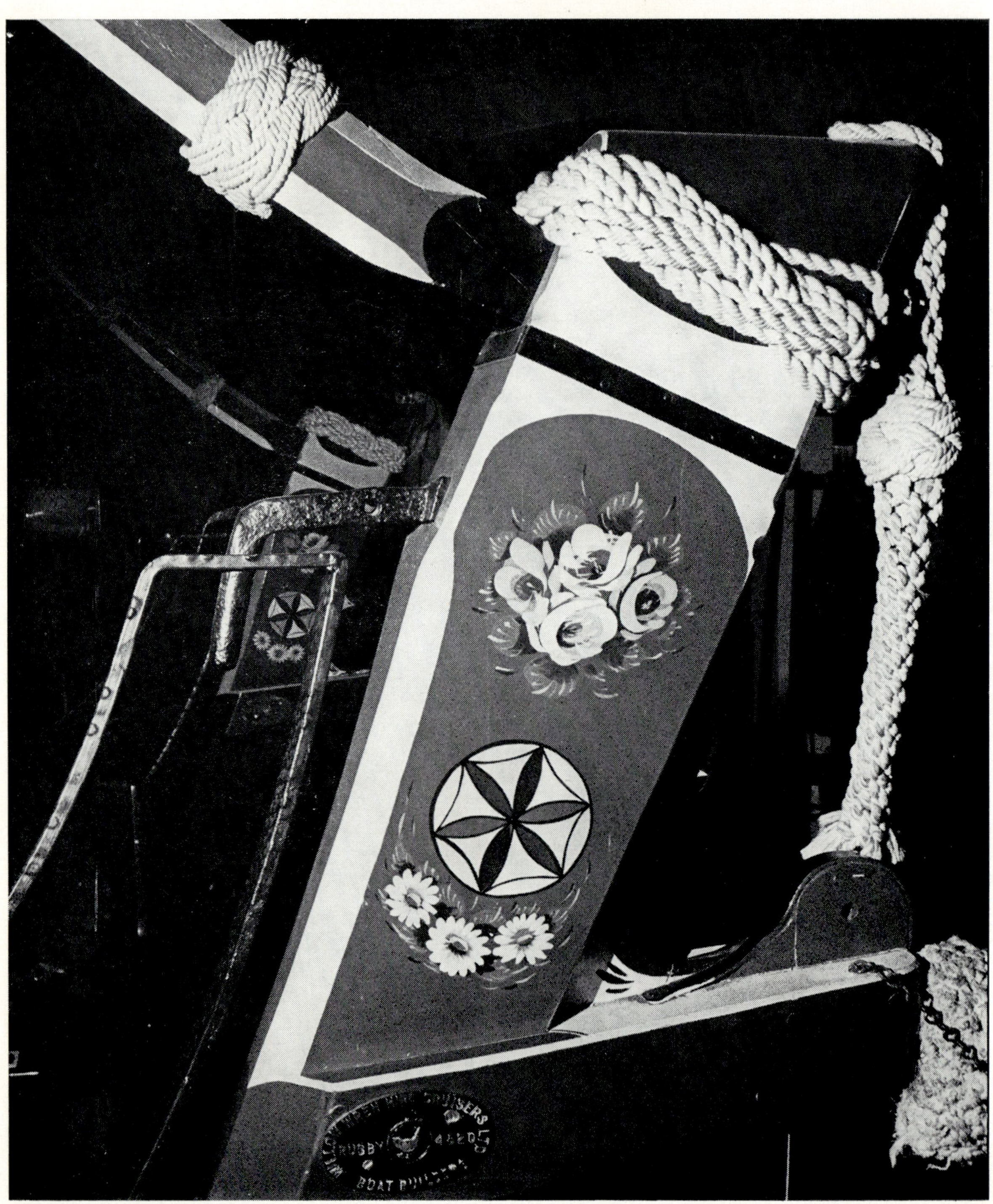

Details of painting on rudder post

Bow and stern ropework fenders

Rare painting of dog on canvas used to decorate interior of stern cabin

Water can and dipper

Decorated water can

Coronation plate

Large teapot. Measham ware

Measham teapot made in the shape of a kettle

Girl's costume, with apron and sun bonnet, *c.* 1858

Traditional boatman's suit, early twentieth century. The shirtfront is patterned with stitched featherwork

Traditional costume of canal boaters

Harnessed canal horse with coloured bobbins, nose bowl, decorative brasses and ear stalls

1. Boatman's bucket
2. Large can
3. Small can
4. Stool
5. Nose bowl

Painting cans and utensils

The painting of water cans and similar items in the round is in some ways more exacting than decorating the structural surfaces of a narrow boat. Similar roses and castles are painted on cans as on any other part of the boat, although roses are more frequently in demand.

In addition to the smaller scale and less rewarding surface agent, the painting of articles in the round is inhibited by rounded contours, changes in angles of slope and by awkward corners. The only guide lines used are a few chalk marks and those produced by a miniature snap line, although the position of spout, handle and other features enables the painter to check on symmetry and correct placing of centre lines.

Although it is possible in theory to work on any primed surface the most suitable for cans and dippers is a form of tinplate. This consists of thinly rolled plates of iron or mild steel dipped in molten tin. Tinplate is not measured or gauged in the same way as other sheet metals, its thickness being expressed by strength marks in the form of crosses shown as IX, XX and XXX. One cross is approximately equal to 27 standard wire gauge and mainly used for small utensils. Larger cans are made from three cross tinplate, equal to 26 swg. The handle of the can is usually a pressed steel fitting in the south and a round wire handle in the north, the latter having a handgrip of turned wood or a hollow section of bamboo cane.

Galvanised metal cans have been used for a number of years; they are factory rather than craftsman made products and are considered by the purist to be unsuitable for painting. To paint successfully on galvanised surfaces the painter has to treat the metal with etching fluid. Paint adheres better to tinplate than to other metals but unfortunately tinsmiths

Water can (southern type)

Water can (northern type)

are now few in number and their products in short supply.

A typical water can found on the cabin roof of a narrow boat and chained to the stovepipe as a safety measure would be of five, four or three gallon sizes. Different parts are painted with different patterns and motifs. Handles and spouts are often striped while the lid and sides are painted with alternating bands or swags of roses and daisies. Some larger cans have a painting of a castle in the centre-front beneath the spout, while others are decorated with either the name of the boat or its owner and the date of painting. Perhaps the most successful designs are floral, using leaves and greenery as space fillers. A band at the bottom of the can is often painted with diagonal stripes, similar to spout and handle. The underside of the can is left undecorated.

Flowers are painted in near-natural colours but with a stylised or formal approach. Daisies have white or coloured petals surrounding red or yellow centres. Roses are red, pink or yellow and less frequently white. White roses painted against a blue background are mainly popular in the south, especially in the London area and on waterways connected with the Thames. Deeper shades are represented by darker or brighter colours, while highlights, to emphasise the curl of leaf or petal, are in light colours, often white. Leaves are usually filling or spacing materials and finely pointed to contrast with the fuller, rounder shapes of blossoms. Veining and shading of leaves may be picked out with deft strokes of the brush. Brush marks which seem to have been dabbed in almost at random, space fillers in their own right, surround each group of leaves and blossoms at the outer edges.

Having made the surface to be worked over free from dirt and grease, the painter applies an undercoat. This is either grey or white, sometimes in bands or patches of both colours. White underpainting is applied where bright red over tints are needed. Background colours may be bottle green or Prussian blue, less frequently red, yellow or black. The heart or centre of the flower is painted first, either as a disc or filbert shape. Outer petals are added later, each petal forming a single, emphatic brush mark. For this purpose a filbert-shaped brush may be used, spread out under a slight but definite pressure. Bristle marks of each stroke add a feeling of liveliness and rhythm to the painting as a whole.

While there are about seven petals to each rose, a daisy has up to 20 petals. It is unnecessary to be accurate but either too few or too many produce a lifeless, overcrowded or ill-balanced effect.

In order of painting, flower centres are followed by petals and later surrounded by leaves. Stalks, stems and tendrils are usually omitted. Shadow masses are put in first and highlights added later. Veins of leaves also serve as highlights on some foliage, the centre vein being fine and narrow while outer veins are pointed towards the centre and thicken at the outer edges. Each line of light colour is frequently stressed or repeated by a complementary darker line.

Other items and utensils painted in the traditional style include dippers, nose cans or feeding bowls and ordinary buckets; the latter, known as 'boatmen's buckets', have become something of a rarity on narrow boats during recent years. Boatmen's buckets were mainly used for taking large quantities of water from pump, well or spring in the days before stand pipes were commonplace. The undersides of dippers and nose cans are painted with either roses or castles, usually roses, while the undersides of watercans and buckets are left undecorated. This is because nose cans and dippers (frequently called hand bowls in the north) are turned upside down on the cabin roof when not in use, displaying the undersides. Bucket and water can however both rest on their own firm bases, seldom displayed for more than a few seconds at a time and not worth decorating.

Perhaps the most riotous and fecund display of roses appears on the sides of the boatmen's bucket, two separate bunches or swags with at least 14 mixed roses and daisies appearing in each bunch. A similar number might also appear on the bottom of the nose can as a single bunch. The underside of a dipper has a group of about six roses and daisies with daisies round the outer edge or foot and a continuous garland of about 20 large roses and daisies round the outside of the container.

Painting furniture and interiors

Nesting stools used in stern cabins of canal boats as portable furnishings are decorated on seat and legs with either roses or castles. The castle design, where this is used, is in the form of a rectangular panel with scalloped edges and corners, having a swag of roses or daisies on each side of the panel. Roses are usually painted on the legs or supporting cross pieces which are also lined out in lighter or darker contrasting colours.

Coal boxes, clothes boxes and similar containers are decorated in a style similar to the above with the emphasis on roses rather than daisies.

Interior walls of cabins are painted in panels of bright colours surrounded by borders of oak graining or are completely grained from floor to ceiling. Complete oak graining has been a more popular style since the 1900s, uncovered surfaces throwing back a harsh glare of varnished browns and yellows. Perhaps the most outstanding feature of interior decoration is the raised flap of the crock cupboard. This is a deep panel with a rounded top protecting the front of a china cabinet but letting down at meal times from the vertical to the horizontal, having a leg or underprop for safety. The exterior, when raised, displays a fine landscape enclosed within a frame-like moulding. Sprays of roses ornament the rounded space above the centre panel, other floral motifs clustering round the edges of the moulding and setting off the cupboards and drawers beneath the table area. A further castle, but sometimes a swag of roses or a simple heart shape contained within a dark red moulding, decorates the door leading into cargo space or engine hole. Other flowers fill up odd corners while the panel of the folding bed, known as the 'bed hole piece' (covering the bed hole) often displays an extensive landscape. The flaps of some bed hole pieces frequently have two panels which on account of reduced scale are more likely to contain flowers than landscapes.

Even the interior of the engine hole and the exterior of the fuel tank are given the full treatment of roses and daisies. Roses also ornament seat boards and ticket drawers.

When not covered by lino, floors are painted or stained in strong primary colours, often red. Additional interior colour is provided by painted surfaces of stools, containers, the lacy patterns of beribboned curtains, glazed pottery and brass ornaments.

The double doors of the cockpit are usually made with three panels each on the inside, the outer surfaces being flush with the exterior bulkhead. Top panels have small paintings of castles or farmhouses; centre panels have floral designs and lower panels are left plain. Lower panels are often reinforced with metal plates ('kick plates') to protect woodwork from accidental kicks and scratches. The surround or framework of each door is grained to match the stern cabin interior. While top panels are superimposed above the door frame, as though added at a later stage of construction, lower panels are deeply recessed.

Smaller painted items displayed in the cabin interiors include tea trays, tea caddies, tobacco jars or tins, sugar tins and biscuit boxes or barrels. Most of these containers, which tend to be rounded rather than square or rectangular, are secured with neat brass locks, the keys to which are in the safe keeping of the boater's wife.

Familiar liveries of the past 30 years

British Waterways *Blue and yellow*

Grand Union Canal Company *Red and blue*

Cowburn and Cowper *Red, green and yellow*

Willow Wren *Red, yellow, green and blue*

Thomas Clayton *Red and green*

Fellows, Morton and Clayton *Black and white, or red and green*

Stevens and Keay Limited *Black, red and white*

Midlands and Coast *Red, blue, yellow and green*

Thos Bantocks *Chocolate and cream*

Blue Line Cruisers Limited *Blue, white, yellow and red*

T.S. Elements *Red, green and yellow*

Chapter 5 Ropework and Cordage

Ropework and cordage, essential features of life on the inland waterways, have practical uses almost without number. Most varieties were formerly produced in the once numerous canalside factories, noted for their long covered sheds or rope walks. Although ropes have been associated with almost everything afloat since time immemorial it was on the canal narrow boat that their decorative possibilities were first widely exploited in Britain. Even when some of the ropework ceased to be of practical value it was retained in the positions known to former generations. Although some boaters bleach or pipeclay their ropes the effect of almost dazzling whiteness is usually attained by hard scrubbing, a treatment also applied to various items of canvas cloth and the protective covers over name bands and stern decks.

The most outstanding feature of ornamental ropework is to be found on the rudder post or ram's head. This forms two intertwined bands, above and below the tiller, each known as a 'Turk's head'. While the upper Turk's head consists of four separate cords the lower is usually of three. With a stretch of the imagination these bands may be said to resemble the headgear of ancient Turkish warriors from which the name derives. The name applies more to pattern of weave than to position and function, as Turk's heads may also be seen on other parts of the boat, especially the tiller. Some were used, though less frequently, to bind the top of the rudder blade. Fag ends of rope or cord are often coiled and neatly inserted under interwoven bands between wood and rope.

A vertical length of interwoven cord connects the top of the ram's head with the rudder blade and is known as the 'swan's neck'. This has loops at each end with a wider bulbous part in the centre where spliced strands are woven round a short length of polished wood. Some have either one or two miniature Turk's heads decorating the bulbous section. Spliced and woven cords also connect the pintles of the rudder with the stern post; they resemble ornate and enlarged versions of the lanyards formerly worn by mounted troops of the British army.

Hanging ornaments of knotted or woven cord appear on the box mast and cabin stovepipe, also at the exterior corners of cabin bulkheads where they are known as plaited 'side strings'. On most boats the end top planks are secured to their block or the cabin roof by strands of rope of a type which also secures semi-permanent covers on or near the cratch. A neatly coiled rope on the roof of the stern cabin of the butty may have both decorative and practical functions.

Towing ropes on the canals are usually known as 'straps' or 'snubbers' (short or long respectively); they are secured by T-shaped studs. Other ropes in common use are for lowering and raising side cloths above the cargo space or for mooring. Side cloths serve the dual purpose of keeping the cargo dry, especially when passing through locks, and preventing a heaped cargo such as slack or coke from falling out of the boat.

The art of knotting cord, string and spliced rope is said to have originated in the Middle East over a thousand years before Christ. It was used for trimming shawls, camel saddles, decorative hangings and for a variety of other purposes. During the eighteenth century it became fashionable in England, having crossed the Channel from France and southern Europe. Sailors of the period often employed their leisure hours making 'sennits' or decorative objects of braided cord from which the ornaments of narrow boats may have derived. Known as 'macramé' or 'macramé lace' this type of ornamental work was popular with the Victorians who revived it for trimming shelves and curtains. As a form of string knitting it could also be used for making belts, waistbands, outer vests and other garments. Although appearing complex at first sight, work of this type requires no special skill beyond the knowledge of a few simple knots and raw material of firmly twisted manufacture such as cord or string.

Fenders of coiled rope appear at various strategic intervals on the narrow boat to protect both structure and paintwork. The largest of these are the bow and stern fenders, larger on the motor boat than on the butty. Many butty boats are without a stern fender abaft the rudder blade. Fenders are often made from the frayed or unwanted rope ends stored in the fore cabin or stern locker. Worn parts fill interiors while better quality rope binds the outer surfaces or edges. Manilla appears to be the most popular form of traditional cordage.

Chapter 6 Boaters' Ornaments

In dealing with the decorations and furnishings of narrow boats it is frequently difficult to distinguish between what is ornamental and what is practical. While functional items are also admired for their ornamental effect many decorative pieces are at least suitable for daily use, although they are seldom if ever pressed into service. This is particularly true of the china and crockery in which the boater's wife takes considerable pride.

The most outstanding items of crockery are 'Measham ware', now collected by enthusiasts as 'barge ware' although not always confined to canals and sometimes in evidence at Sunday school tea parties. It was produced in several commercial potteries in the Swadlingcote-Church Gresley area. Similar work has also been traced to Burton-on-Trent. The main producers were Mason, Cash and Company Limited of Church Gresley, not far from the terminus of the Ashby Canal (the Moira Cut). This was within the borders of Derbyshire, a few miles north of the Leicestershire village of Measham which later became a terminus of the Ashby Canal until navigation was further curtailed at Donisthorpe.

This type of ware was still in vogue until the late 1930s, although the first recorded items appeared during the early 1870s. Leicester Museum has records of an item dated 1874. Although Measham ware is still used and collected manufacture appears to have ceased during the Second World War. Orders for this barge ware were usually placed at a canalside shop adjacent to the Georgian warehouses at Measham Wharf. They were forwarded to the pottery and the finished ware returned in due course bearing personal messages and names stamped on the sides. They were usually secured by a small down payment, known as 'a shilling in advance', and collected when the boater next visited the area. Identical ware inscribed with mottoes and texts was also manufactured for suburban housewives.

Urn-like teapots known as 'barge teapots' are the main objects of interest. The largest of these might hold well over a gallon, or about 16 cups of tea, reflecting the average boater's fondness for this beverage. Most teapots have a knob above the lid in the form of a miniature teapot in replica; these however are easy to break and very few survive intact, mostly having chipped spouts or missing handles. As an alternative to the replica some teapots have knobs in the form of over-sized acorns. Other popular items include milk or cream jugs, teapots made to resemble kettles, sugar bowls, flower vases (usually in pairs) and tobacco jars. Nearly all teapots have a toothed rim under the lid. On the whole earlier types tend to be smaller, plainer and lighter in colouring, a few having straight sides and plain rims. Many teapots have matching stands but these seldom survive and few appear together in modern times.

Characteristic features of Measham ware are moulded outer decorations in pastel colours, with bands of lettering in black on white, contrasting with a shining treacle-brown background. Ornaments include birds (pheasants), baskets of flowers, horns of plenty, individual leaves, flowers and blossom heads. Early teapots tend to have fewer mouldings, and these restricted to flowers and fruit. The dark brown glaze, almost black on some examples, was applied over a yellow under-body which resembled 'the cane coloured clay from Lount'. It was described as a mixture containing raw lead carbonate, normally free from cracking and crazing after firing. Its depth of tone and lustre is fairly uniform although some items are much lighter than others and inclined to be mottled.

Many examples are wedding gifts or commemorate anniversaries and other special occasions. Teapots appear to take pride of place but flower vases are seldom seen on canal boats. They are often handed down like family heirlooms from mother to daughter. It is claimed that barge ware was used on the waterways long after it ceased to be fashionable in the suburbs, mainly because of the boater's innate conservatism and love of tradition for its own sake. Interest in it is now widely shared a second time, prices for Measham ware in good condition having reached an impressive level during the 1960s.

Other familiar items of pottery include blue Staffordshire ware, some decorated with willow pattern designs, others with stylised views of canalside scenery. The Waterways Museum at Stoke Bruerne has an interesting example of a blue and white serving dish with views of Woolstanton, a pottery village on the main line of the Trent and Mersey Canal.

Staffordshire milk jug

Pottery figures of Staffordshire origin have long been commonplace in crock cupboards and on corner shelves, noted for rude vigour of execution rather than for delicate artistry. They are mainly portrait figures or animal models, either 'flat backs' or 'all-rounds'. Some of the earlier figures depicted popular heroes and heroines, of real life or literature: members of the royal family, Rob Roy, Garibaldi, Florence Nightingale and Napoleon III. Wellington and Sir Robert Peel may have survived from an earlier generation but the most popular figures belonged to a later era. The characters they depicted were not all harmless celebrities; crooks and murderers such as William Corder of *The Murder in the Red Barn* and James Rush the Wymondham assassin were among them. Some models are in the form of a group or tableau representing such exciting moments as a 'rescue', 'flight' or 'arrest', a popular theme being a struggle between police or gamekeepers and armed poachers. Staffordshire animal models are usually over-simplified and sentimental. The most frequently encountered are lapdogs such as miniature spaniels, usually sold and displayed in pairs. These have goggle-eyed, soulful expressions and are ornamented with elaborate chains, lockets and collars. Wild animals of a more exotic type, such as lions and tigers, were formerly seen in the crock cupboard but less frequently than dogs. A typical survivor from the early Victorian period was a milk jug in the form of a cow, its tail twisted into a handle and the spout predictably hidden between the front teeth.

Plates and other items of souvenir chinaware have always been popular with canal folk, in stern cabin and lockside cottage. They are often lace-edged with open-work patterns, or frets and bars, through which brightly coloured ribbons might be threaded. Rows of plates hang in tiers from floor to ceiling where space allows. Noted for a wide range of pictorial motifs, they depict landscapes, views of seaside resorts, capital cities, country villages and gothic churches. Vertical motifs such as lighthouses, windmills and even Blackpool tower may further emphasise the need for increased headroom and living space. Other popular designs are still-life compositions with over-ripe fruit and waxen flowers. Less familiar themes, dating from the earlier days, include portraits of individuals, or several figures grouped together illustrating story or legend, usually head and shoulder views with scornful hero and simpering heroine. Generals and other military heroes of the Boer War were also popular for a short time, including Baden-Powell, Lord Kitchener, General Roberts and General Buller. It is unlikely that lace plates have ever been specially made for canal dwellers as it appears they are frequently bought secondhand, either from market stalls or canalside shops. Many were of Bohemian origin, from a part of Czechoslovakia then within the bounds of the Austrian empire. The popular manufacturing firm of Schumann, exporting during the 1900s, was located in Bavaria. Large numbers of plates and similar ornaments are merely stamped 'Foreign' and may have come from any part of central Europe. It may be noted that Measham products were always unstamped, without distinguishing marks or labels of any type.

Pictorial motifs on lace plates are frequently obscured by burnished windlass handles, either full-sized or miniatures, hung in front of each plate. These are decorative rather than functional, secured with a bow of the same ribbon threaded between the frets. Many plates are inscribed with the motto 'A Present from Ramsgate', or some other resort, printed in gothic letters.

Goss china was a favourite ornament of the late nineteenth and early twentieth centuries. This was produced for many years in the Stoke-on-Trent factory of William and Henry Goss. It was mainly souvenir ware, coloured red, green and blue on pure white, often taking the form of tiny shoes, gloves, bottles or miniature sailing ships, each bearing the civic arms and motto of the city or borough where it was intended to be sold. During the First World War there was even a miniature submarine in Goss ware.

Tea trays were fairly common ornaments before the First World War. They were made from a variety of materials, ranging from ordinary wood and metal to Japanned ware. Large numbers of imitation Japanned trays were produced in the Birmingham area from the mid-nineteenth century, especially in the factories of Messrs Jennens and Betteridge.

Brass and copper ornaments run china a close second in popularity. These metals are kept in a high state of polish throughout the year and rarely allowed to grow dull or tarnished. The glowing state of brightwork was long held to be a test of a boater's character and origins, distinguishing a genuine canal family from a mere 'Rodney boater' or 'bird of passage'. External brass ornament is mainly in evidence on the stovepipe chimney, which is frequently bound with two or three 'rims'. Stovepipes may be removed for cleaning or for passing under low obstructions; the chain securing them to the cabin roof was an elaborate piece of brasswork stapled to boss-shaped ornaments. Similar bosses, either whorl or star-shaped, are fixed to cabin bulkheads on each side of the double doors or in any space where additional ornament is thought to be necessary. During the Second World War safety chains were made from the hooks and rings of military webbing equipment as it appeared in war surplus shops.

Brass rails and knobs, even small bells, are widely used in stern cabins, especially near the stove area. The top of the stove has a protective rail and there are also brass rails secured to the ceiling directly above. A brass or copper damper sleeve edged with filigree work covers the upper part of the stovepipe below deck level. In later years the combined cooking and heating range was frequently replaced by a small heater and separate cooker run on bottled gas. Some cabins have a gas cooker and a coal or coke stove, the latter using the same chimney as the earlier range.

Other familiar items of brass or copper ware are oil lamps and their brackets, candlesticks, large copper kettles and

Typical horse brasses

many cooking utensils such as copper colanders, and pots and pans.

Brass ornaments in the crock cupboards may include miniature windlass handles, spoons, toasting forks, crudely modelled human figures and small animals. Small brass monkeys and elephants are popular in the round, frequently worn down by constant polishing to appear almost rudimentary. Horse brasses are displayed in groups or fixed to side walls and panels as individual items. They include all varieties from dolphins to sheaves of corn and geometrical figures. Most are mounted on a leather harness strap such as a martingale.

Flat cabin brasses are fixed to wall spaces, usually at a fairly high level. They are often in the form of portrait busts, figures or animals, but riding horses and military chargers are among the more popular subjects. A fascinating pair appeared in 1911 at the time of the coronation of George V. Known as 'The King's Horse' and 'The Queen's Horse', they could be found on many narrow boats of the period. 'The King's Horse' was a heavyweight hunter with a bang tail and hogged mane, wearing a severe bit and standing martingale. 'The Queen's Horse' was a more attractive animal but on a smaller scale, an Arab or Barb of the palfrey type, with tasselled bridle, embroidered saddlecloth and elaborate holsters. Tail and mane were wavy and flowing in the best traditions, repeating the elegant curve of poll and crest.

Crochet work was a favourite pastime of many boat-women, the finished products being used for a variety of purposes. In former times it was mainly used to oranament and trim women's shawls or other garments. After the 1920s however it was used almost exclusively for trimming cup-boards, shelves and curtains. Edges or borders were finished with coloured tassels spaced at regular intervals. The ear protectors worn by canal horses to ward off flies in hot weather were often crocheted by the boater's wife or daughter. Crochet work also covers birdcages displayed on stern cabin roofs.

Many boaters are versatile craftsmen, able to turn their hands to a variety of odd jobs from running repairs to painting a tea tray or door panel. Some fill up their limited spare time making cabin stools, often from scraps of driftwood, of which there are ample quantities in or near canals. While most stools may be used as cabin furniture some are small enough, being no larger than matchboxes, to make souvenirs or toys for children. Other boaters have tried their skill at modelling their own craft, the model eventually appearing with Goss ware and china dogs in the crock cupboard. Making string belts and smacking whips were also popular diversions up to the time of the Second World War. Smacking whips were cracked not to drive horses but, before the days of brass-mounted fog horns, as a warning near tunnels and bridge holes. Lashes for the whips were sold in most canalside shops.

Tools used by boaters are few and simple, but patience, ingenuity and a steady hand make up for a lathe, a vice or an elaborate workbench.

Chapter 7 Traditional Dress

The traditional dress of canal families was worn by many boaters and their wives up to the Second World War, though it was less frequently seen in daily life after the mid-1920s. In later years it was mainly reserved for Sunday best or special occasions rather than working days.

Men wore two main versions, the more popular being a finger-length coat or jacket with velvet collar and revers, corduroy trousers, white or striped shirts with pleated fronts stitched in feathered patterns of coloured silks, woven string belts or braided and embroidered braces and heavy boots. Younger men frequently dispensed with jackets, working in their shirt sleeves, especially in summer. A neck-cloth or choker, often a form of coloured handkerchief similar to a 'Belcher', were worn in place of tie or cravat. Trousers were fairly narrow but cut in naval style with bell bottoms. Most shirts had buttons made of bone.

The alternative style was similar in several of its features, embroidered shirt, string belt and braces being universal. It was usually a two-piece suit, though sometimes worn with a waistcoat of corduroy or self-material. Cord waistcoats fre-

Traditional costume. (*Left to right*) Moleskin waistcoat, bonnet and shawl, and two-piece suit with piped edges

quently had brass buttons. Dark colours in a small check pattern were preferred to large checks, stripes or houndstooth. The edges of the jacket and waistcoat were trimmed with narrow braid or piping, on collar, cuffs and pocket flaps. Jacket cuffs might be turned back about six inches from the wrist. There were at least five pockets, including a hare pocket, and a single back pleat or vent. Boaters were usually fussy about details and accessories so that false buttonholes and pleats were unknown. Waistcoats and other garments were sometimes made of moleskin.

A narrow leather belt with a polished brass buckle was frequently worn round the waist by both men and women. Into it might be thrust a windlass handle for opening lock gates. With men the leather belt might be worn in addition to the ornamental string belt. Men, and less frequently women, carried short smacking whips with plaited thongs. These hung down the outside of trouser leg or skirt on the right side but under the jacket and looped through the belt. They would be worn, even on power boats, either for show or to crack as a warning signal. The average smacking whip had a round handle about ten inches long ornamented with horizontal coloured bands. Thongs, of spiral weave, varied in length and were much longer in the north than the south.

String belts were fairly deep, like cummerbunds. They were fastened at either front or back with twin leather straps and brass buckles. Being of double thickness they could also serve as a spare pocket or wallet. Weave patterns were usually assorted squares or dice shapes trimmed with coloured embroidery. Strands of wool or silk thread were interwoven with the strings of both belts and braces.

Men's headgear was usually a peaked cap. The cap varied in size and style, those of the 1900s appearing to project at back and sides. Many boaters before the 1870s appeared to favour the billycock hat, and some early caps had smooth or shiny peaks. From the late 1930s the trilby and porkpie hat began to make an appearance, but the bowler was almost unknown at any period, despite its many revivals by landsmen. Trilby hats whatever their original style or degree of smartness soon lose shape in all-weather conditions and often give the latter-day boater a somewhat battered, trampish appearance.

On northern canals the men wore wooden clogs tipped with brass. Lighter footwear of the same style, similar to dancing clogs, would be worn for special occasions.

From the 1920s there was a general decline in sartorial standards. The decline reflected the fact that fewer master-men were at work on the canals, most of the once proud owner-boaters being forced to sell their craft to large carrying companies. To lose independence and take a cut in one's general standard of living was obviously a great blow to self-confidence, especially when the policy of larger companies was to survive through strict economy. As a result of longer working hours and a less hopeful future, men who had once taken great pride in their appearance began to look shabby and down at heel.

The costume worn by women on the canals was virtually unchanged for many years. Unlike their sisters on the land they were probably more conservative in such matters than their menfolk. Long, full skirts and small, often 'handspan', waists survived far longer on the inland waterways than elsewhere. Clothing tended to be dark and plain, especially after the 1880s; dark clothes were associated in the minds of the Victorians with respectability. Striped or flower-sprigged patterns were not entirely unknown, especially for summer wear, but they were far from typical. Apart from the small waist, clothes followed natural lines, with separate bodice and skirt as the main outer garments. A yoked effect of bodices or blouses might serve to emphasise sloping shoulders and small waist lines, both considered highly feminine. The throat was frequently enclosed by a high or stand collar fastened with a brooch and sometimes stiffened with whalebone. Sleeves were full and bagged at the elbows but enclosed at the wrists with neat cuffs. Most women wore a long white or black apron tied at the back with a bow knot; it had deep hems and a starched waistband. While matrons and those of mature years wore their skirts below the ankles, younger girls and unmarried women wore them slightly shorter.

Headgear was often the traditional sun bonnet, once familiar in hay and harvest fields of many country districts. It was pleated, crimped and goffered, with long ribbons on each side reaching down to the waist and either left to hang

Traditional bonnet

or tied under the chin. A distinctive feature of the bonnet was a deep neck ruffle, sometimes extending the length of a cape. This was admirable protection in all weathers, especially when steering in the semi-open cockpit of a butty boat. During the 1900s certain boatwomen in the south wore broad-brimmed or straw hats with dark ostrich feathers or floral decorations. On the northern canals women and girls frequently wore head shawls. Deeply fringed shawls had been worn about the shoulders from the 1840s.

Footwear for women varied from light pumps to high lace-up boots, enclosing the lower part of the leg from instep to mid-calf. These were high heeled, of dark soft leather and more frequently black than brown. The uppers of some boots extended to the knees.

As with men, standards of women's dress began to decline during the inter-war years. Within the space of a decade most women began to adopt a more modern style of costume, which if less charming was certainly more practical and in keeping with the times. Skirts rapidly became much shorter for women of all ages; skirt and bodice were replaced by skirt and jumper or blouse. Long aprons were less frequently worn, replaced during working hours by a sleeveless pinafore-style garment in floral patterns. Ordinary shoes with cross straps, plimsolls or gumboots were worn in place of lace-up boots. A brimless hat or beret replaced the sun bonnet and a few women even wore men's hats or caps.

During the Second World War head scarves and turbans made their appearance on the canals when these fashions became popular in the Land Army and among women factory workers. Such utilitarian garments as jeans, sweaters and dungarees have been popular with both sexes since the end of the war.

There was no particular style of dress for children, apart from short skirts for girls and short trousers or knickerbockers for boys. The main trends, as in other walks of life, were for girls to lengthen their skirts and raise their hair as they grew older while boys graduated to shorter hair and long trousers. Both sexes tended to lead a ragged, half wild existence except when they were crammed into stiff collars, black stockings and starched pinafores for special occasions. Many ran barefoot in summer, the boys without jackets; boys and girls both tended to wear much-darned jumpers in cold weather.

Boatwomen frequently made their own clothes and the shirts of their menfolk. Some specialised in making elaborately pleated blouses which they sold among their friends or through canalside shops with which they might have an arrangement. Towards the end of the last century smartly dressed boaters of both sexes seemed to have much in common with the costermongers of the East End of London. It is generally considered that the boaters originating from the London area or working over the canals of the home counties were the leaders of taste and fashion on the canals.

Chapter 8 Lettering on Boats and Buildings

The style of lettering on canal boats is an impressive feature of their external design. Side panels of cabins, recording details of the carrying company or owner, plus registration numbers, usually bore a plainer sans-serif than the lettering style used for the name at the stern. Though the name of a boat may be shown at both stem and stern, it appears to greater advantage on an inward and upward curving band extending from the gunwales near the after bulkhead to the stern post. This tapers towards the rudder so that the lettering diminishes and loses two or three inches of height between first and last letters. The name of the firm or owner is usually upright; the name of the boat often slants italic-style.

At the turn of the century, lettering on the side panels of stern cabins often had the top line in the form of an arc or bow and lower lines usually straight.

Filling details, such as swags of roses or arabesques, are much in evidence on side panels, especially on those of power boats the counter sterns of which are unsuitable for decorative work or much detail. A motor boat's name appeared on a side panel rather than at the stern.

Most lettering is in a freelance, full-blooded style, its face described as 'Ionic', with blocked and curved serifs. Style tends to be exaggerated both in the shape of serifs and in the contrasts between thick and thin strokes or bars. Much lettering, on both stern and side panels, has considerable depth of shading; this applies equally to serif and sans-serif styles. Some shadow areas are worked out with elaborate lining and highlights, producing an almost three dimensional effect known to boaters as 'shadowgraph'. Lower case or small lettering is almost unknown, except for registration numbers and details of addresses. A cursive style similar to

Canal boat lettering

handwriting was frequently used on the former Barlow boats, the first letter in each word being larger than the following letters.

Colour schemes usually run to light pigments on a darker ground, although the order might be reversed in the case of small end panels containing boat number, registration number and town of origin. In later years the registration number had by law to be shown in black on white, but this is now no longer necessary.

Lettering on canalside buildings, bridge plates, signs and notices followed the more conservative trends of the day but tended towards Roman or Egyptian rather than gothic styles. Names and signs on canalside inns were especially pleasing, although a decline in craftsmanship and desire to seem modern at all costs now leads either to neglect or to repainting in less attractive styles.

The original styles of lettering on canal craft and buildings, often freehand with the minimum of planning, usually harmonised with their surroundings in form, scale and texture. Although decorative and frequently lacking uniformity, the styles were at least clear and legible enough to read without strain from a considerable distance. It is essential however to think of the finest boat lettering as a kind of handwriting rather than a kind of print. Measurements were seldom made, the only aids being a chalked string and sometimes a flimsy lath or batten curved to produce an arc. Lettering produced by an early generation of boaters was sometimes inconsistent, not only in its use of thick and thin strokes but also in the shapes and directions of such letters as S, E or F, many of which were painted back to front.

Chapter 9 Horses and Harness

Horses, mules and donkeys played an important part in the life of the canals for at least 170 years. Although still found in odd corners of the inland waterways, but only occasionally in regular employment, horses declined in numbers and importance from the late 1920s while mules and donkeys have almost completely disappeared from the scene. However, the narrow boat *Gifford* was mule-drawn up to 1971, and Joe Skinner of the *Friendship* remained faithful to mules for many years after the Second World War.

Horses were usually preferred to other animals for their superior strength and comparative docility. Although mules were frequently used, especially up to the mid-nineteenth century, they were inclined to be cross-grained and unpredictable. Donkeys needed to be worked in pairs and took up more room on the towing path than a single larger beast. Normally quiet, willing and even-tempered, donkeys were known to have fits of stubbornness when nothing short of gross ill treatment would make them budge. Yet even the horse, like most livestock, needed understanding (something quite different from misplaced kindness) for full co-operation. During 1905 the Shropshire Union Canal Company, one of the largest carriers on its own system, owned 328 horses, over 200 more than any other firm. Stables would be

A canal horse in traditional harness

found at all the main canal centres, also forges for shoeing, barns for fodder and harness repair shops. A typical stable on the Shropshire Union Canal was at Bunbury in Cheshire; there were stalls for 22 horses, and a loose box which may have been used for sick animals.

The last stronghold of donkeys, known to boaters as 'animals', was on the Worcester and Birmingham Canal, over which they worked between the heart of industrial Birmingham and Diglis Basin a mile above Worcester bridge. They almost vanished between the wars; mules lasted another 20 years, mainly on branch canals away from the busier main lines.

The Oxford Canal was one of the last waterways to be worked almost entirely by horses, although a fair number of day boats on the Birmingham Navigations and the Staffordshire and Worcestershire Canal were drawn by stocky cob-like horses, or those of a small 'vanner' type, until after the Second World War. In the central area of Birmingham they were used for many years to assist both power boats and butties through difficult lock flights. Horses were on the way out long before the Second World War on the Grand Union Canal, although a number were retained for barge traffic on wider sections at the London end until they were replaced by small tractors during the early 1960s.

Horse getting into draught

Types of horses varied according to the waterways and the craft and cargo handled. The navigations called broad or barge canals, in common with river navigations, depended more on heavy shires, up to and above 16 hands (a hand = 4 in.), than on cobs or vanners. Shire horses are the hairy-heeled giants once familiar in the drays of railway and cartage companies or on farms. They are still used by some of the larger brewery firms and for showing by enthusiasts. On the narrow or boat canals more compact horses were needed, ranging from the all-purpose cob type to ex-carriage or riding horses fallen on less happy days. Some were even former racehorses and noted for their speed and willingness, proving the value of bloodstock even when it is in reduced circumstances. Massive shires were rather ungainly on narrow towing paths or passing under low bridges and would have been out of their element on many of the Midland or northern canals. In some ways smaller horses were hardier than larger types, returning better service and longer hours of work for the same amount of forage. They were better able to endure extremes of heat and cold than shires and less prone to suffer from complaints of the feet and legs for which the feather or fetlock of shire horses, harbouring damp and grease, was largely to blame.

Horses kept after the 1920s were seldom required to pull more than one boat at a time, so that muscular power was less important than stamina. While the shire could move record-breaking loads it needed more rest and refreshment in proportion to size than other types.

The working gear of canal horses was trace harness, often seeming as varied and colourful as the decoration of the boats they hauled. The flanks of the horses were protected from chafing ropes by wooden rollers known as 'bobbins'; about 20 of these were threaded to each rope on either side of the horse, between neck collar and swingletree or stretcher. They were egg-shaped and usually painted in a scheme of at least three different colours, such as yellow, blue and red, with a colour for each bobbin. Less frequently a leather sleeve was used in place of bobbins. Stretcher, swingletree and the hames of the collar were painted in horizontal bands of vivid colours.

Stretchers were flat or round bars of wood attached to the

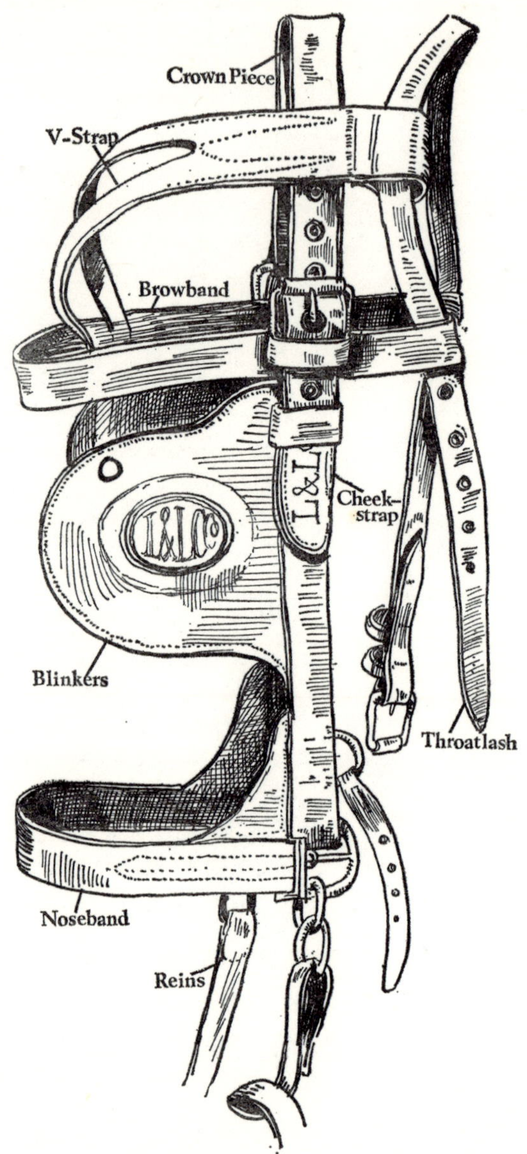

Bridle worn by horses on Leeds and Liverpool Canal

rear part of the harness by strap and buckle. Lines secured to the towing rope were fixed to staples at each end of the bar. Used during the early days of horse-towing, they were retained on the northern canals long after they ceased to be used in other parts of the country.

The swingletree was a curved or bow-shaped towing bar of either light or heavy pattern, sometimes having a centre pivot. The attachment for the rope was a single hook in the centre of the bar. The length of a towing rope was about 100 feet.

Several of the more important harness straps were ornamented with heart-shaped studs of solid brass, while a broad strap or martingale between the forelegs was loaded down with at least six brasses. All harness buckles were brass, kept in a high state of polish; they were oval or round rather than square or oblong. A small brass plate or disc on the centre of each blinker or eye piece of the bridle would have the name of the owner or the initials and symbol of the carrying company engraved in ornamental letters.

Hames, or the curved metal bars of the neck collar, were much shorter than on ordinary draught harness to prevent scraping against the arches of bridges and tunnels. Although the bridle was fitted with a bit and reins these were seldom used, the bit hanging under the chin and reins tied to the top of the hames. An experienced horse needed very little guiding or restraint and soon learned to obey spoken commands from the boat. Some which had the irritating and sometimes dangerous habit of snapping wore cage-like muzzles of leather straps which also prevented them from stopping to crop grass.

A solitary brass ornament, suspended in the centre of the forehead a little lower than the eyes, was known as a 'face piece'. There might also be a whorl-shaped ornament on each side of the head at the junction of brow band and cheek straps on the bridle. This was called the 'rosette'. Other brasses were mainly suspended from the martingale. Horse brasses are of great antiquity, even pagan origin, and are thought to have been worn as amulets by all beasts of burden to ward off the evil eye. They have many variations in different parts of the country, although the most popular have long been the crescent moon with star, the sun-in-his-glory, whorl shapes and pointed shields. Later more sophisticated designs include windmills, running foxes, the elephant and castle and even railway locomotives. The finest examples date from the first half of the nineteenth century, but there have been many fakes and most of those now in circulation are of fairly recent origin.

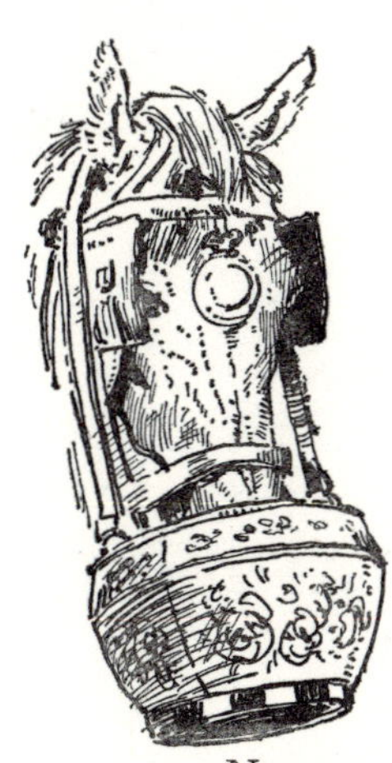

Nose can

The celebrated horse bowl or nose can, worn so that the horse might feed at convenient intervals without being led to a manger, replaced the canvas nosebag of other draught horses. It was about 8–9½ in. deep and 10 in. in diameter widening by 4 in. from the inside top. External surfaces, including both sides and base, were painted with roses and castles, usually the former. When not in use the bowl was either hung by a leather strap from the hames, or displayed on the cabin roof. Some canal horses were fed from cane baskets rather than nose cans.

Ear protectors were glove-like coverings or stalls; they had deeply fringed sections hiding poll and forehead. Coloured tassels trimmed the borders and hung from cords on both sides of the animal's face and head.

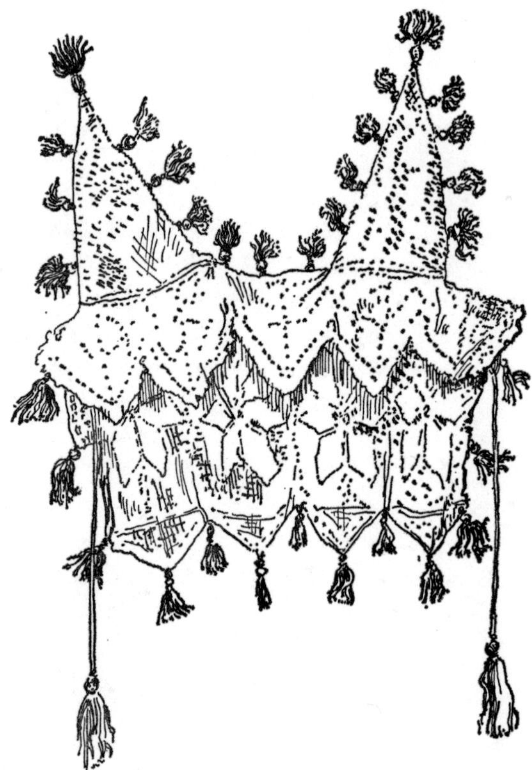

Ear protector for horse or mule

Appendix Canal Boat Population

According to a booklet by J. B. Hutchins, *The Law Relating to the Registration and use of Canal Boats as Dwellings, Comprising the Canal Boats Act of 1877 — The Regulations of the Local Government Board and the Board's Instructional Circular*, published in 1878, the number of persons living in canal boats during 1861 was 11,915 consisting of 8,494 males and 3,421 females. This was based on reports made by a Mr Baker and his colleague Captain May of H.M. Government Factories Department. No account was taken of boatmen on rivers and other waterways.

Mr Baker refers to the writings of Mr George Smith of Coalville, Leicestershire, who claimed (in 1876) that 80,000 to 100,000 men, women and children were living, sleeping and working in connection with boating. 'There would be an average of four boats per mile on four thousand eight hundred (4,800) miles of rivers and canals.' This would make the number of boats to be 19,200; supposing there to be a man and woman and three children connected with each boat, there would be a total of 96,000 women and children.

Numbers of boats and those living on them gradually declined during the next hundred years. By the early 1960s the British Inland Waterways Board was operating approximately 70 pairs of narrow boats — in trade — with families of varying sizes living on board. The Board has now ceased to operate their own fleet apart from a few repair boats — none of the latter being family boats. Since this abandonment decline has been even greater and it is no longer legally necessary to register boats with local authorities. Although a small number of families still live on narrow boats many of the craft are used infrequently, considered as houseboats rather than a means of livelihood.

Should there be a revival of commercial boating it is anticipated that this would be either through day boats or the employment of hired crews.

Glossary Terms used in connection with canals and boats

Back door Communicating door of a stern cabin in narrow boats, between living quarters and cargo space.

Barge Craft mainly used on broad canals (barge canals) or navigable rivers; more than 7 ft. beam.

Barge master Captain or skipper of a barge.

Bargee Crewman or owner-skipper of a barge; the term later applied to all men working boats or barges over the inland waterways.

Bed hole Cupboard in the stern cabin of a narrow boat in which the cross bunk or bed was concealed during day-time; usually had cupboards above and drawers under.

Bench bunk Side bunk in the stern cabin of a narrow boat.

Boat Canal narrow boat with less than 7 ft. beam.

Boat captain Skipper of a narrow boat.

Boater Person of either sex living or working on a canal boat.

Boatman's bucket Large painted bucket used as a water container; frequently used before the introduction of stand pipes and water cans.

Bottle stove Bottle-shaped stove widely used for heating in stern cabins of narrow boats; were eventually replaced by a patent heating and cooking range with side ovens.

Bowhauliers Men working in teams to haul boats or barges on inland waterways.

Box mast Square-shaped telescopic mast of a narrow boat; used both for towing and to support the top planks.

Bracket lamp Oil lamp in the stern cabin of a narrow boat fixed to a side wall or bulkhead by means of an ornamental bracket; usually made of brass.

Breasting-up Securing two or more boats side by side; done for mooring, passing through double locks or when being towed by a river tug.

Bridge plate Oval or oblong metal plate above the arch of a canal over-bridge recording the number and sometimes the name of the bridge.

Bulk Bulbous ornamental structure of canvas stuffed with hay or straw on a framework of wood; attached to the cratch or front board of a narrow boat for decoration.

Butty Former horse boat; the non-powered, towed boat of a working pair.

Cabin block Wedge-shaped wooden block on the roof of a stern cabin; used to support the final top plank of the upper gangway.

Carvel build Popular method of narrow boat and barge construction; side planks of the hull are fixed edge to edge instead of overlapping.

Catcher Hook-shaped anchor used on narrow boats either in time of flood or when navigating rivers without proper mooring facilities.

Chalico Protective dressing of cowhair, tar and horse dung smeared over the wooden parts of a canal boat.

Coal box Painted box used to contain the domestic fuel supply in the stern cabin of a narrow boat; frequently used as a step down from the cockpit.

Cockpit Opening, guarded by top slide and double doors, forming an entrance to the stern cabin of a butty.

Composite boat Narrow boat constructed from the late 1920s with steel side plates and wooden bottom.

Counter Flat, rounded stern of a motor or power boat.

Cratch Triangular front board near the prow of a narrow boat used to support top planks and side cloths; connects with a hollow after structure known as the false cratch.

Crock cupboard Open-fronted cupboard in a stern cabin protected by the raised flap of a folding table; used for the display of china ornaments and other items.

Cross bunk Main double bed in the stern cabin lowered from a side cupboard or bed hole; occupies a space in the forward half of cabin, blocking back door when in position.

Day boat Narrow boat without living quarters mainly used in the Birmingham area; worked on an out and back principle in daytime stints; also known as a 'Joey boat'.

Deck lid Hinged cover opening above the fore cabin or storage locker.

Dipper Shallow water container with a short wooden handle; kept on the roof of the stern cabin when not in use beside mop and water can.

Elum Combined tiller and rudder of a butty boat.

Engine hole Engine space on a motor or power boat.

Family boat Narrow boat with accommodation in stern and fore cabins for the boater and his family; much favoured after the 1850s.

Fender Protective pad or buffer slung over the side of a boat or barge to prevent damage to either boat or moorings; made of old or unused ropes.

Fish spear Barbed spear or trident used for catching fish and eels.

Fly boat Swift canal craft working express services between important centres; often given right of way at locks and bridge holes; frequently worked at night.

Fore cabin Small cabin containing a cross bunk in the fore part of certain narrow boats.

Gunwale Also gunnel (pronounced gun'l); the upper edge or top side of a boat or ship above the waterline; so named as cannon on early warships were fired above the 'whale' or upper line.

Hatches Welldeck in the stern of a butty between steerage and cockpit.

Horse boat Narrow boat towed by a horse or mule; term also used for a certain type of raft or pontoon used to ferry horses across rivers or broad canals.

Joey boater Crewman of a day boat or 'Joey boat'.

Keelson Long shallow keel of a narrow boat, without which the craft would be flat-bottomed.

Lock wheeler Person who rides or runs ahead of a narrow boat to open the next lock.

Long boat West country or west Midland name for a narrow boat.

Long bottoms Long wooden planks used in constructing the bottoms of wooden or composite boats.

Mast box Lower section of the box mast (*qv*); used to contain the telescopic upper section.

Monkey boat Name used in the London area and later the Midlands for a narrow boat.

Monkey box Container for cleaning materials on a narrow boat.

Mop Rag mop the handle of which is decorated with colourful stripes.

Motor boat Power boat or tug of a working pair.

Navigation lamp Same as a tunnel lamp; usually fixed to the upper part of the cratch.

Navvies From navigators; workmen responsible for constructing the navigation canals; later employed on railway and road work.

Nose can Also known as a nose tin or nose bowl; feeding can used by canal horses and mules in place of a nose-bag.

Number one Owner-boater; few survived the depression of the late 1920s.

Oakum Spliced rope dressed with hot pitch used for sealing between the planks of a boat.

Owner-boater see 'number one'.

Packet boat Passenger boat also used for the conveyance of packages and parcels.

Pigeon box Box-shaped ventilator above the engine hole of a motor boat.

Ram's head Rudder post of a horse boat or butty.

Rims Brass bands round the stovepipe chimney of a narrow boat.

Rodney boat Neglected family boat; a floating slum of the inland waterways.

Running blocks Round-topped wooden blocks used for guiding a towing rope; fixed above the cargo space of a narrow boat.

Shafting Punting a boat by using a long shaft or pole.

Shearings Thin oak panels or planks which line the interior of a wooden-hulled narrow boat.

Side cloths Protective cloths drawn up from the sides of cargo space on a narrow boat.

Side panels Exterior panels on the tumblehome of a stern cabin; used to display registration numbers, the name and address of the owner and decorative landscapes.

Slack boards Also known as 'wash boards'; planks used with a cargo of slack or small coal to prevent it washing overboard and to increase cargo space at the stern end of the hold.

Slide Hatch cover over the cockpit of a stern cabin.

Smacking whip Whip carried by boaters to smack or crack as a warning signal before the introduction of horns or sirens.

Soap hole Round hole or cupboard near the cockpit entrance of a stern cabin.

Stands Flat, attenuated upright supports secured through slots in stretchers; with the box mast and cratch they support top planks.

Starvationer Cigar-shaped narrow boat used in the underground workings of certain drift mines and on the Bridgewater Canal; double-ended, 24 ft. in length; so named on account of narrow or starved appearance.

Stern cabin The main living quarters on a family boat.

Stretchers Cross planks used to strengthen the structure of the hull or hold on a narrow boat.

Struts Narrow sections of wood sloping inwards from the gunwale of a narrow boat; used to assist in the support of top planks and side cloths.

Swan's neck Ornamental ropework connecting rudder blade with ram's head on a butty boat.

Ticket drawer Shallow drawer near the cockpit entrance of a narrow boat containing lock passes.

Tiller Curved wooden beam used for steering a boat or barge; on a motor boat is a Z-shaped steel rod, often with a brass extension.

Top cloths Protective cloths raised from the gunwales or lowered from above the top planks; mainly used to protect perishable cargoes.

Top planks A gangway of planks supported by mast, stands and struts; extending from end to end of the cargo space on a narrow boat or from cratch to cabin.

Towing path Specially constructed path alongside a river or canal; used by beasts of burden for towing boats and barges; originally known as the 'haling path'.

Towing post Same as box mast.

Tumblehome Inward sloping sides of the stern cabin on a narrow boat.

Tunnel cutter Metal ring or hoop above the funnel of a power boat; used to break up smoke and fumes in a tunnel or bridge hole; also to protect the funnel from falling soot or plaster.

Tunnel lamp Large oil lamp suspended near or from the cratch of a narrow boat; made with either a straight or curved lens; now replaced by electric lamps as used on motor vehicles.

Turk's head Ornamental ropework, spliced and woven; used to decorate the ram's head and other parts of a narrow boat; said to resemble the turban of an ancient Turkish warrior.

Water can Large drinking water container with hinged lid, spout and cross handle; usually kept on the roof of the stern cabin alongside dipper, mop and boat hook.

Waterman Boatman or bargee.

Windlass L-shaped tool used by boaters for opening paddles on lock gates; also known as a 'windlass handle'; often carried in the belt.

Windlass hole Small cupboard in the stern cabin of a butty containing a windlass and spares.

Decorative items used by boaters

Barge ware Name under which Measham ware is collected in modern times.

Crochet work Form of knitting with hooked needles known as 'crochet pins'; produced by womenfolk of boaters in their spare time; used as interior trimmings or as ear stalls for canal horses, etc.

Goss china Small china ornaments frequently displayed by boaters in the crock cupboards of stern cabins; sold as souvenirs of certain towns, especially seaside resorts.

Horse brasses Harness ornaments originally worn by draught horses as a good luck token or to ward off the evil eye; collected by boaters for display in stern cabins.

Lace plates Ornamental plates collected by boaters for display on the interior walls of stern cabins; noted for their fretted borders made with lace-like patterns; usually hung in vertical rows threaded on lengths of coloured ribbon. Mainly produced in countries of central Europe.

Measham ware Ornamental tea urns and similar items, salt-glazed in dark glossy colours; produced in factories at Swadlingcote and Church Gresley; originally sold to boaters in a shop at Measham Wharf.

Staffordshire ware Blue and white plates, dishes and tea services, either designed with the familiar willow pattern or local views; also highly glazed figurines of human figures or animals.

Terms used in connection with painting boats and utensils

Agent Surface to which paint is applied, *eg*: wood, canvas, metal.

Arabesque Pattern of sweeping curves, often painted on the bulkhead of stern cabins.

Brushes Used for either painting canal boats or utensils such as water cans and dippers; of several different sizes, grades and types; small hair brushes are used for fine details on cans while larger bristle brushes are preferred for external panels.

Brushwork Pattern of brush strokes or bristle marks; imparts a feeling of liveliness and spontaneity to most oil paintings, especially on wooden surfaces; cannot be traced when the medium is too thin or moist; boat painters used brushwork with almost subconscious skill, mainly to emphasise form, contour and direction; much of the apparent vigour of the best canal painting springs from uninhibited brushwork.

Combing Technique used in graining to produce wavy lines of light colour contrasting with darker tones.

Compass wheel Motif similar to petals of a flower, radiating from a centre but contained within the circumference of a circle.

Copal varnish Distilled and prepared from the resin of certain tropical trees or shrubs; used as a protective transparent layer during the final stages of graining.

Filler Space filler, such as leaf or petal, introduced to improve composition; from the viewpoint of design and layout a mean should be found between dull voids and overcrowding; this entails balancing space against the objects it surrounds.

Flower Lighter parts in graining picked out with a small piece of clean rag.

Good luck symbols or tokens Motifs such as the four-leafed clover, ace of clubs or Staffordshire knot, displayed on decklids, slides or side panels of canal craft.

Graining Technique of staining intended to simulate the

grain of either light or dark oak.

Graining comb Comb of wood, card, metal or other suitable material; see 'combing'.

Highlight The lightest or brightest part of a painted object, often throwing back a reflected light such as ripples on water or gloss on polished surfaces struck by direct light; such passages are usually thickly painted (impasto), while shade and shadow are laid on with thinner, leaner tones; boat painters showed great skill in their use of impasto, relating this to confident brushwork; the introduction of highlights combined with depth of shadow is ideal for producing an effect of solidity and three dimensions.

Knotting Filling up knot holes in woodwork before painting.

Lining out Pattern of painted outlines repeating the forms and outer contours of structural features on canal boats and utensils.

Linseed oil Oil from crushed flax seed; used in the basic grinding, preparation and application of oil-based paint; the use of too much linseed oil, while imparting a temporary brilliance, causes a painting to turn yellow and darken prematurely; poppy oil is a better alternative but far too expensive and difficult to obtain for the average boat painter.

Mahlstick Long stick with a cloth-covered knob at one end, often used by professional painters as a hand rest; useful in painting fine details; seldom used by boat painters.

Palette A convenient flat surface, usually polished wood, used for mixing, blending and testing paints before application; the range of pigments used is also termed a palette.

Primary colours Three basic colours, red, blue and yellow, from which all others are derived, *eg*: blue + yellow = green.

Primer The first coat of paint applied directly to the surface or agent.

Scotch plaid Pattern of coloured cube and dice, similar to tartan; used in ornamenting external surfaces of narrow boats.

Sepia tint In narrow boat painting a semi-transparent tint of warm brown (sometimes brown mixed with black) used for shading or outlining, especially when depicting landscapes.

Shapes Geometrical or abstract patterns and designs painted on the structural parts of narrow boats; mainly diamonds, squares and compass wheels (*qv*).

Snap string or line Chalk-covered string made taut and secured at both ends; when wanged against a flat surface leaves a straight line for use as a guide, mainly for lettering or lining out purposes.

Stopping Filling large cracks in woodwork before or during painting.

Turpentine Spirit distilled from balsam or resin obtained from certain conifers; mixed with paint to dilute or thin the medium during application; preserves the original colours and is less likely to darken or discolour than linseed oil; excessive amounts however give work a dull or dried out appearance; some painters mix turpentine with linseed or poppy oil as a vehicle.

Vehicle The thinner or medium used to dilute paint and make it more tractable.

Terms used in lettering

Cursive style Letters joined together in the style of handwriting.

Egyptian style Debased style of Roman lettering with bold, crude forms; widely used during the first half of the nineteenth century.

Roman style Lettering based on examples used by the ancient Romans, especially on monuments and triumphal arches; noted for mainly thick vertical and diagonal strokes plus the use of serifs.

Sans-serif Lettering in plain or block form without the addition of serifs.

Shadowgraph Shaded letters with a three dimensional effect.

Upper case Capital letters.

Harness for boat horses and mules

Blinkers Eye shields worn by most British draught horses but less frequently seen on the continent; in theory a horse, having its eyes placed partly at the front and partly at the sides of the head can see backwards with the tail of the eye; a young or mettlesome horse could thus be alarmed by the glimpse of an object drawn behind and might bolt.

Bobbins Brightly coloured wooden rollers worn by canal horses and mules to prevent chafing of harness against the flanks.

Bridle Head straps forming attachment for bit and reins.

Collar The usual collar for canal horses is the standard draught or neck collar favoured in the British Isles, as opposed to the breast collar and harness worn mainly on the continent and in later years adapted for military purposes; the neck collar is better suited to the heavier types of horse bred in England and in general stands up to rough usage better than the breast collar, which is designed for quicker, lighter work; its main drawback lies in the need for accurate and comfortable fit to avoid galling of neck and upper shoulders. Collars are made of firm but flexible leather, padded, lined and stuffed with straw; adjustments are sometimes made by altering the padding.

Ear protectors Stalls of crochet work worn by boat horses and mules in summer to protect the inner ear from insects.

Face piece Round brass ornament worn by a canal horse or mule in the centre of the forehead; two smaller pieces were sometimes worn instead of one large piece.

Gear Same as harness or tackle (tack); term for the harness of horses and mules, mainly used on the canals.

Hames Curved metal bars on the neck collar of a draught horse; fit into grooves between the fore and after parts of the collar (wales), forming attachment for trace bars or hooks; upper terminations of the hames, fairly low on boat harness, project above the level of the collar on each side but curve towards the centre.

Martingale Harness strap between the forelegs of a draught horse connecting collar with girth; formerly loaded with brasses, mainly crescent-shaped.

Rosette Rounded or disc-shaped ornament worn as part of the bridle at the junction of brow band, cheek straps, crown piece and throat lash.

Stretcher Horizontal bar used as part of trace harness for canal horses and mules, to which the towing rope was connected by means of staples at each end; similar to the spreader of normal trace horse gear.

Swingletree A later development of the stretcher; usually curved, sometimes with a central pivot; towing line is attached to a central hook rather than by leads to end staples; similar to the wipple tree of three horse tackle.

Trace harness Form of draught harness; different from cart harness in having more lines and chains in place of leather straps; often known to farmers as 'working in chains', the extra horse of a pair in tandem being termed the 'chain horse'; harness for the average carthorse means attachment to shafts with a heavy cart saddle, breeching strap about the hindquarters and numerous hooks and chains for attachment to the shafts; trace harness is for work without shaft or pole and would be used for towing boats, barges, railway wagons or tubs, ploughing, harrowing and timber-hauling; trace harness is mainly worn when it is impossible to bring the horse near to its load and towing from a distance is required; this applies equally to a boat on a waterway, some distance from the bank, a harrow dragged through rather than over the surface of the ground, or anything not supported by a set of wheels.

Bibliography

Aickman, Robert *Know Your Waterways*, London, 1955

Calvert, Roger *Inland Waterways of Britain*, London, 1963

Chaplain, Tom *A Short History of the Narrow Boat*, 1967

Chappell, Metius *British Engineers*, London, 1942

Cranfield & Bonfiel *Waterways Atlas of the British Isles*, London, 1966

Edwards, Lewis *Inland Waterways of Great Britain and Ireland*, 1950

Hadfield, Charles *British Canals*, London, 1950; New York, 1950

Harris, Robert *Canals and Their Architecture*, London, 1969

Malet, Hugh *The Canal Duke*, London, 1965

Maré, Eric de *Canals of England*, London, 1955

McKnight, Hugh *Canal and River Craft in Pictures*, London, 1969

Priestley, Joseph *Historical Accounts of the Navigable Rivers, Canals and Railways Throughout Great Britain*, London, 1831

Rolt, L. T. C. *The Inland Waterways of England*, London, 1950; New York, 1950

Rolt, L. T. C. *Narrow Boat*, London, 1944

Salis, H. R. de *Bradshaw's Guide to the Canals and Navigable Rivers of England and Wales*, London, 1904

Index